IN OLD PHOTOGR

BRITAI

ABERGAVENNY

PAST & PRESENT

I.M. MORGAN

SUTTON PUBLISHING

in association with ABERGAVENNY LOCAL HISTORY SOCIETY

Sutton Publishing Limited
Phoenix Mill · Thrupp · Stroud
Gloucestershire · GL5 2BU

First published 2003

Copyright © I.M. Morgan, 2003

Title page photograph: The clock tower at
Abergavenny Town Hall. (*Trevor Scott*)

British Library Cataloguing in Publication Data
A catalogue record for this book is available from the
British Library.

ISBN 0-7509-3378-X

Typeset in 10.5/13.5 Photina.
Typesetting and origination by
Sutton Publishing Limited.
Printed and bound in England by
J.H. Haynes & Co. Ltd, Sparkford.

To my Mother and Father

The Llanvihangel to Hereford tram road bridge over the River Usk looking towards the Skirrid
Fawr, also known as the Holy Mountain, shown in an 1829 print by Henry Gastineau. The
medieval bridge is shown behind. (*Abergavenny Museum*)

CONTENTS

Abergavenny Borough Council was granted a coat of arms on 27 March 1901, two years after Queen Victoria renewed the town's charter. The Marquess of Abergavenny had been influential in supporting the application for the charter and the armorial bearings are based on his coat of arms. His family, the Nevilles (now the Nevills), have been Lords of Abergavenny since the fifteenth century.

The motto 'Hostes nunc amici' means 'My enemies are now my friends'. This relates to the reconciliation between the town and the Crown through the 1899 renewal of the charter. The charter had been revoked in 1689 after the town's Roman Catholic burgesses refused to swear allegiance to King William and Queen Mary. Abergavenny had previously been granted charters by Henry VIII, Charles I and Oliver Cromwell.

The shield has two golden fleurs-de-lis which are said to derive from those on the arms of the ancient Kingdom of Gwent. The fleur-de-lis symbol is also found on the insignia of the town's seventeenth-century corporation and the seal of the nineteenth-century Improvement Commissioners, forerunners of today's Monmouthshire County Council. The shield also has a portcullis which the Nevills used as a badge.

The borough's crest, a pied bull, is the same as the Marquess's, except that the borough arms also has a tree which is sprouting on the one side. (*Oswald Jones*)

A BRIEF HISTORY OF ABERGAVENNY

The attractive market town of Abergavenny in the valley of the River Usk is set against a dramatic backdrop of hills which form the southern end of the Black Mountains. It lies at the point where the Gavenny river joins the Usk. The Welsh word 'aber' means mouth of the river. Gavenny is probably derived from the British name Gobannia, 'the river of the iron smith'. The modern Welsh word for smith is 'gof'.

This historic town, dominated by the Blorenge, Sugar Loaf and Skirrid Mountains, stands at the eastern gateway to the Brecon Beacons National Park. It is surrounded by lush pasturelands in stark contrast to the rugged beauty of the Beacons on one side and the once industrialised valley towns on the other.

Above: A view of Abergavenny from the castle looking towards the Sugar Loaf Mountain, including the Town Hall on the right and St John's tower in the centre. (*I.M. Morgan*)

Right: Where two rivers meet . . . the Gavenny joins the Usk. (*S. Morgan*)

Looking down Frogmore Street towards the junction of Lion Street and High Street in the early 1900s. (*Abergavenny Museum*)

The importance of one such industrial neighbour, the town of Blaenavon, was recognised in the year 2000 when it was awarded World Heritage status. The Blaenavon Industrial Landscape site also covers the Blorenge with its early tramroad built to provide access to the picturesque Monmouthshire–Brecon canal which follows the contours of the mountain. Within the heritage site, too, are the rural villages of Llanfoist and Govilon (see the meaning of 'gof', above) which lie on the outskirts of Abergavenny.

Abergavenny and its surroundings are a major attraction for tourists who want to visit the ancient castles, priories and churches, and also for sports enthusiasts interested in outdoor pursuits such as walking, horse-riding, paragliding, fishing and canal boating.

The town lies on what would have been the southern edges of a massive ice field during the Ice Age. Glaciers scooped out the U-shaped valleys of the Usk and Llanthony and deposited mounds of fluvio-glacial sand and gravel further down. Abergavenny was built on one such bluff. Glacial action also formed the hollow on the north of the Blorenge and the one known as the Punch Bowl on its east side.

The underlying geology is the St Maughan's formation of old red sandstone of the Devonian period, some 400 million years ago. Limestone is found on the Blorenge, Gilwern Hill, Mynydd Llangynidr and Mynydd Llangattock, an area well known for its cave networks.

There is rich evidence of human activity dating back to the late Palaeolithic or Old Stone Age, the period about 12000 BC. Archaeologist Frank Olding describes Abergavenny as sitting in one of the most remarkable prehistoric landscapes in the British Isles.

Axe found at Llantilio Pertholey on display at Abergavenny Museum. (*Ken Key*)

Flint tools found on the Sugar Loaf probably show where hunter-gatherers made their summer hunting camps in the Mesolithic or Middle Stone Age (*c.* 10000–4500 BC). Excavations have shown that there was a flint working area at what is now Flannel Street and tools have been found at Blaengavenny Farm. These finds indicate the sites of winter camps made on valley floors. Excavations at Gwernvale, near Crickhowell, uncovered the site of a Neolithic community dating from about 3900 BC when farming was introduced. The first large-scale ritual monuments, the Black Mountains chambered tombs, were built about this time.

A number of excavations, including nine by the Abergavenny Archaeological Society between the 1960s and '80s, have helped to unravel some of the mysteries of the different periods in the town's past. In one dig on the Flannel Street site (now the post office) a sherd of late Neolithic pottery was found (*c.* 3000 BC).

A flint arrowhead and other worked

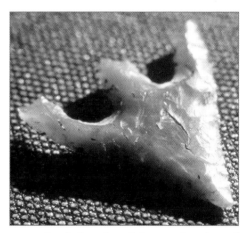

Arrowhead flint found during the Flannel Street dig on display at Abergavenny Museum. (*Ken Key*)

flints were unearthed on the sewerage site which suggest that there was a small settlement by the river. Excavations at an upland site on the slopes of the Sugar Loaf called Y Graig, once thought only to date from the early eighteenth century, have uncovered flint tools dating from the Mesolithic, Neolithic and Early Bronze Age times.

Standing stones, stone circles and round burial cairns on the ridges of the Black Mountains date back to the Early Bronze Age (*c.* 2500 BC) when farmers and shepherds began to clear upland forests for summer grazing. The Flannel Street dig unearthed a fine flint arrowhead from this time.

The uplands were abandoned during the Middle Bronze Age (about 1200 BC) after the climate worsened and it became colder and wetter. Life must have become harder which lead to warfare between groups. Weapons have been found dating

The Marquess of Abergavenny opens the town's new library in 1906. Among the guests was the Lord Mayor of London. Look out for the foundation stone, laid the previous year, which spells Abergavenny with three 'n's. (*Abergavenny Museum*)

from this time such as a sword at Pen Tir near Cwm Du and swords, spears and axes at Llantilio Pertholey.

A tribal Celtic culture emerged during the Iron Age (*c.* 750 BC–AD 43) and the people would have spoken Brittonic, a forerunner of Welsh. Gwent and Glamorgan were controlled by the Silures while the Dobunni ruled what is now Herefordshire. Villages and hill-forts were built at strategic sites like Pentwyn, Twyn-y-Gaer, Table Mountain and Walterstone. It is thought that the Silures conquered the Twyn-y-Gaer area between 390–200 BC.

The Romans reached Abergavenny between AD 55 and AD 57. They built a fort – on what is now the Castle Street car park – called Gobannium. From the Latinised name, it is likely that they found some iron working in the area.

Gobannium was part of a chain of strongholds linked by roads developed by Didius Gallus, the governor of Britain, to conquer the fierce Silures. The fort was probably constructed by a detachment of the Twentieth Legion from the new legionary fortress at Usk before being garrisoned by a troop of auxiliary cavalry or a part-mounted legionary cohort. The Second Augustan Legion built the new legionary fortress at Caerleon in AD 74–5, about the time when the Silures were finally subdued. Gobannium may have been used as a workshop and store depot for that campaign.

Roman forts were usually constructed to a standardised pattern. They were rectangular with rounded corners, four gateways set in turf and timber ramparts,

Roman artefacts at Abergavenny
Museum, including a jar and querns
for grinding corn. (*Trevor Scott*)

Jars and two Roman cremation urns on display at Abergavenny Museum. (*Trevor Scott*)

and a ditch or ditches. The Castle Street dig uncovered a pair of back-to-back, half-timbered barrack blocks with glazed windows facing a granary across what may have been the Via Principalis, the fort's main road.

Other finds included fragments of legionary armour, chain-mail and horse harnesses, so both legionary troops and a cavalry unit could have been stationed at Gobannium in the first century AD. Crucibles and scrap bronze found at Flannel Street indicate a military workshop.

A 1964 excavation at the Abergavenny post office site established the west ditch and gateway of the fort. The 1972 dig at the Orchard site behind Castle Street revealed a section of the south-west turf and timber ramparts. Pieces of samian-ware pottery and sling stones were found at Castle Street. Two delicate brooches, one in the shape of a dolphin, have been discovered. Other items were recovered from a rubbish-tip at the foot of a steep incline outside the fort. Coins have turned up in Cross Street, near Hereford Road, Pen-y-pound and at Mardy.

Gobannium was rebuilt a few times. Firstly by troops of the Second Augustan Legion in about AD 100 and then again about fifty years later when it was given a new layout and a stone-built bath-house which stood in what is now Plantagenet Court. A brick stamped LEG II AVG was discovered near Abergavenny Castle. The main Roman cemetery was along Bailey Park and the Hereford Road. An urn from a Roman burial was found there and is now at the National Museum of Wales. Part of another urn, from Park Crescent, is on display at Abergavenny Museum.

In about AD 250, the fort's defences were refurbished for the last time. Forts usually had small civilian settlements, called *vici* (singular *vicus*), outside their walls and one may have survived at Abergavenny for a time as a market and trading centre after the fort had been abandoned. Coins have been found dating from between AD 393 and 400, and this probably marks the end of Roman rule.

In the fifth century, after the Romans had left, new Welsh kingdoms began to emerge during the fight against Saxon invaders from the east of Britain. The first of these kingdoms was Gwent, the northern part of which was called Gwent Uwchcoed and included the Abergavenny area. In about AD 600 this was controlled by Iddon ab Ynyr, king of Gwent.

The seventh-century *Book of Llandaff* records that King Iddon gave land in Llantilio Pertholey to the church. One clause, in Old Welsh, lists all the features along the parish boundary but it does not mention a settlement there.

The Normans arrived in Gwent towards the end of the eleventh century. The first castle they built in Wales was at Chepstow (known then as Striguil) which they started in 1067, less than a year after the Battle of Hastings. The Normans used Chepstow Castle, incidentally the first stone castle in Britain, as a springboard to push back the frontiers in the Welsh and English borderlands, in what became known as the Welsh Marches. They started to build earth and timber castles at strategic points in an attempt to subdue the native population. The first Abergavenny castle was built in about 1087 by the Norman lord Hamelin de Ballon, and was a motte and bailey wooden castle. The site at the south-east point of the glacial mound

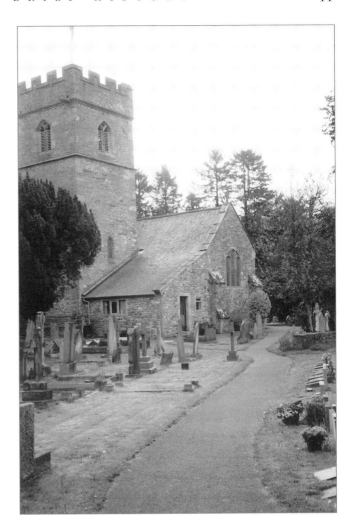

St Teilo's Church at Llantilio
Pertholey was built on a
seventh-century site.
(*I.M. Morgan*)

was adjacent to the one the Romans had chosen nearly a thousand years before and from where the Normans, too, could control the river crossing and routes to other strongholds.

De Ballon also set up the Benedictine priory of St Mary's, a daughter house of the French St Vincent and St Lawrence Abbey in Le Mans. His new town, called Bergavenny, grew up alongside the castle, extending along the present Castle Street as far as the middle of the car park. An embankment and ditch probably defended the town on that side.

The tensions between the Norman invaders and the Welsh frequently broke out in skirmishes and ambushes, leading up to the infamous Christmas Day massacre of Welsh chieftains at Abergavenny Castle in 1175. The Normans immediately followed this by riding out to the home of one murdered chieftain Sitsyllt (Seisyll) ap Dyfnwal at Castell Arnallt, and carrying out another massacre, killing his young son and taking his wife prisoner. The Welsh took their revenge seven years later.

The Gorsedd stones from the 1913 National Eisteddfod at Abergavenny at their new resting place in Swan Meadows. (*Trevor Scott*)

In 1241 the town was extended and protected by a strong, defensive wall with a ditch on the north and the east sides. The rebuilding of the town and castle walls in stone probably started at the end of the thirteenth century. Livestock markets would have been held in the vicinity of what is now Nevill Street. Then came a period of devastation for the town. First came the Black Death which reached Abergavenny by December 1348 and had such an effect that in 1349 officials were only able to collect a third of the rents in the lordship of Abergavenny. Other outbreaks ravaged Gwent Uwchcoed and probably affected the town over the following years.

The beginning of the fifteenth century brought Owain Glyndwr's Welsh war of independence. The Welsh armies besieged the town, burning parts of it, but the castle held out. It took some years before the town of Abergavenny eventually recovered. Henry VIII, whose great uncle, Jasper Tudor, had earlier been granted the lordship of Abergavenny, ordered the burgesses of the town to carry out the rebuilding.

After the dissolution of the monasteries, St Mary's Priory became the parish church and St John's Church became redundant. In 1542 Henry VIII granted a charter which included the right to turn the St John's building into the town's grammar school. The upkeep of the school was financed through tithes which had previously supported the priory.

Abergavenny began to expand and must have become prosperous by this time. John Leland in his 1538 *Itinerary* described it as 'a faire walled towne, well inhabited' and in a description of the county, collected by George Owen in 1602, it was mentioned as 'a fine town, wealthy and thriving, and the very best in the shire'.

During the Civil War, Abergavenny supported the Royalists. In 1645 when a Scots army, fighting for the Parliamentarian cause, arrived in Hereford, the castle at Abergavenny was blown up on the orders of Charles I in a futile attempt to stop Parliamentarians using it as a base.

The town has been granted charters by both Charles I in 1638 – which included control of markets, fairs and the woollen trade – and then Cromwell in 1657. In 1689, however, after the town's Roman Catholic bailiff and recorder refused to swear allegiance to the Protestant King William and Queen Mary, the town lost the royal charter, its borough status and so the right to administer the school. In addition, several tenants took advantage of the situation and did not pay their tithes so that in 1719 the Court of Chancery appointed a receiver to recover them.

During the seventeenth and eighteenth centuries Abergavenny was a centre for industries such as tanning and weaving, and became known for a type of fine Welsh flannel which was named after it. In the mid-eighteenth century the town flourished for a short time as a fashionable health resort. Goats' milk was the prescribed treatment for consumption, and invalids flocked to the town to try the cure. Goat hair was used to make fine white wigs for which the town also became known.

A Great Western Railway bus, passing the Swan Hotel (on the right) makes its way up Cross Street on a busy shopping day in the early years of the twentieth century. (*Abergavenny Museum*)

W.T. Stoneham opened the Argyll Stores at 24 High Street in about 1897. Among the variety of goods on offer was a blend of tea specially selected by a London tea merchant to complement the water in Abergavenny. (*Abergavenny Museum*)

The town became a centre of Welsh culture through the patronage of Lord and Lady Llanover, among others. The Abergavenny Eisteddfod, which played an important part in the development of the National Eisteddfod, was held regularly between 1833 and 1854. Until this time, Welsh was the main language in the area.

By the end of the eighteenth century, the centre of the town needed to be updated. The old market hall built across Cross Street was causing so much congestion that it was eventually demolished and a new one constructed on the site of the present building by the nationally renowned architect John Nash. It, too, was later demolished and replaced by the present Town Hall.

Abergavenny continued to expand with the coming of the railways in the middle of the nineteenth century. Improvement Commissioners – the freeholders who owned more than a certain amount of property – managed the town until 1894. They decided to build a new covered market, and this, with the familiar Town Hall of today, was completed in 1870. Abergavenny finally regained its borough charter in 1899.

The town continued to prosper from its links with the iron and coal industries of its neighbouring valley towns, drawing in day-trippers by the thousand to visit the markets, fairs and the latest attractions at the castle.

In the 1950s and '60s, the council carried out a controversial programme of slum clearances which demolished some of the oldest parts of the town, destroying the heart of closely-knit residential communities. Some pieces from the Tudor buildings were salvaged by townsfolk and preserved at the museum. Fortunately, other ancient buildings have survived, helping the town to retain its traditional character.

One of the largest employers in town is the National Health Service. Nevill Hall is a general hospital serving Abergavenny, the surrounding valley towns and parts of Powys, while Maindiff Court, which is due to be updated, provides mental health services. Pen-y-Fal Hospital (1851–1996) was first built as a joint counties' asylum and at its peak had more than 1,000 patients. Older townspeople still mourn the closure of the small Victoria Cottage Hospital in 1976.

Abergavenny lost its borough status through local government reorganisation in 1974. Now the town is run by Monmouthshire County Council but a mayor is still elected every year from among members of Abergavenny Town Council which bears the town's coat of arms.

A busy Tuesday in the Market Hall. (*I.M. Morgan*)

The Tuesday livestock market, a week after its closure was announced. (*I.M. Morgan*)

New types of markets have been introduced to attract visitors – from craft and antique fairs to flea markets and farmers' markets. The Abergavenny Arts Festival has been entertaining townsfolk and drawing in summer visitors since 1992 and the more recent Abergavenny Food Festival, held in September as a showcase for the best produce in the Welsh Marches, has been an outstanding success.

In 2001, Abergavenny, in common with other British rural communities, was badly hit by the foot-and-mouth epidemic and the livestock market was closed for a time. Then on 29 April 2003 Monmouthshire County Council made a historic and controversial decision to close the livestock market in the town centre, so ending a long tradition. Once the market is moved to an out-of-town location the old site will be redeveloped. The produce and other markets will remain where they are in the Market Hall but a 'piazza-style' development is planned for the Brewery Yard part of the open-air market. Other decisions will also have to be made about the regeneration of the town centre to allow Abergavenny to face up to the challenges of the twenty-first century.

1

Castle & Priory

Abergavenny Castle as it may have looked in about 1100, approximately thirteen
years after it is thought to have been built by Hamelin de Ballon. This was a motte
and bailey castle and the Normans probably used forced labour to dig out a ditch
and pile up the earth inside it to build the huge artificial mound called the motte.
On top of the mound was a timber keep surrounded by a stockade made from
prefabricated pieces of tongue-and-groove planking. This was so that it could be
erected as quickly as possible in case of a sudden attack. At the base of the motte,
another stockade was erected around the courtyard known as the bailey, which had
wooden buildings such as halls, kitchen, sleeping areas, a granary and a smithy. The
keep was connected to the bailey by a 'flying bridge' and the whole structure was
protected by an outer ditch, with a bridge over the ditch. (*Michael Blackmore*)

THE CASTLE

Visit Abergavenny Castle and you will generally find an air of tranquillity which belies its brutal past. The only clash of sword and thud of bowman's arrow will be in a re-enactment or a stage production by a theatre company in the natural amphitheatre on the lawns.

The castle's turbulent history has echoed through the ages. In the sixteenth century William Camden said that it 'has been oftner stain'd with the infamy of treachery, than any other castle in Wales'.

The castle once occupied a strategic position between Wales and England and was the scene of intense power struggles. The Norman overlords in these Marcher borderlands had been granted absolute powers by successive monarchs in a bid to subdue the rebellious natives. At times this led to a three-way battle between the English king, the Marcher lords and Welsh princes, all vying for control.

Abergavenny Castle is most notorious for the Christmas Day massacre in 1175 said to have happened soon after the Norman lord William de Braose inherited the castle. De Braose invited the castle's previous owner, the Welsh chieftain Sitsyllt (Seisyll) ap Dyfnwal, his son Gruffudd and other local leaders to a banquet on the pretext of hearing a royal proclamation.

According to custom, before entering the hall the Welsh had put aside their weapons as a sign of peace. As they were seated at the table, a proclamation was read out forbidding Welshmen to carry arms while travelling. This, naturally, angered the Welsh and at a pre-arranged signal, armed men rushed into the hall and slaughtered them. The Normans then rode out to Sitsyllt's stronghold at Castell Arnallt, captured his wife Gwladus, and killed their seven-year-old son Cadwaladr.

Gerald of Wales tried to explain away this brutality by saying that de Braose had wanted revenge because Sitsyllt had murdered his uncle, Henry, the third son of Miles FitzWalter, Earl of Hereford. Sitsyllt had seized the castle from Henry and controlled it for a time but had been persuaded by his brother-in-law, the powerful Welsh prince, Lord Rhys, to hand it back to the Normans and Henry's heir, William.

Seven years later, the sons and relatives of those murdered chieftains, led by Hywel ap Iorwerth, lord of Caerleon, avenged the massacre in turn by besieging the castle, overcoming the guards and burning down most of it. But, it is said, the keep held out. In 1233, the castle was destroyed by Richard Marshall, so what remains today is likely to be later than that. Murage grants (extra taxes to pay for rebuilding work) were raised in 1241 by William de Canteloupe. The castle's walls at this time were probably still made out of wood. John de Hastings rebuilt the castle and the town walls in stone after getting other murage grants in 1295. His son, also called John, who was responsible for rebuilding the priory church, carried on the work with more grants in 1314.

The Regency hunting lodge, built in about 1819 for the Marquess of Abergavenny on the foundations of the earlier stone keep, was let out as a home and then tea-rooms before it was turned into the Abergavenny Museum. The only remains of the original castle are the motte, now smaller than it used to be, and a length of Norman bank discovered under the east tower in 1990. The original wooden keep was rebuilt in stone, probably between 1150 and 1182. (*Trevor Scott*)

Walk through the gatehouse, and on the right you will see the remains of the Great Hall, the most likely site of the 1175 massacre of the Welsh chieftains. At the time of the massacre, the hall would have been a wooden one. The hall was built at first-floor level and the ground floor would have been used for storage. Two garderobes can be seen in the wall. These were medieval toilets which would have drained into the castle ditch. (*I.M. Morgan*)

Above: This is how the castle might have looked in about 1410. Although much of it was rebuilt in stone, it would have contained wooden buildings such as stables, barns and kitchens. From its earliest beginnings this was an important castle used by kings when they were in the locality. King John visited in 1215. In October 1291 Edward I called a great council of archbishops, bishops, earls, barons and others here to settle a long-running feud between Gilbert de Clare and Humphrey de Bohun. For three weeks the castle was home to the royal court. (*Sally Davis*)

The barbican was probably built to strengthen the castle gatehouse in the early fifteenth century during the Welsh wars of independence led by Owain Glyndwr. The outline of the original round doorway and the arch of the drawbridge can still be seen between the wall and gatehouse. In about 1404 the town was captured and partly burned, but the castle held out. It was still garrisoned throughout 1404–5 by 80 mounted soldiers, their armed servants and 400 archers. (*Trevor Scott*)

An outside view of the south-west towers. At the base is the pit of the garderobe which had to be emptied with a shovel, usually as a punishment for some unfortunate soul. The angled thickening of the lower wall on the south-west towers acted as a defence against undermining and caused missiles dropped from above to ricochet horizontally. (*Trevor Scott*)

Below: The south-west towers, built in about 1300, would have provided sumptuous living quarters for the lord of Abergavenny and his family. The polygonal and round towers would have looked their finest during the late thirteenth and early fourteenth centuries when the castle was owned by the de Hastings family. A circular staircase would have led to a passage by the three large windows on the first floor. The square garderobe tower and outlet can be seen from the outside. (*Trevor Scott*)

The south-west towers and the keep as seen from Castle Meadows by the River Usk. From here you can see the castle illuminated at night under sponsored floodlighting begun in 1985 by Abergavenny Local History Society. Under the scheme, both members and non-members can pay a small sum (£5 in 2003) for a week of their choice to commemorate a birthday or an anniversary with a certificate to keep as a memento. (*Romley Marney*)

The spiral staircase leading to the south-west towers and the luxurious apartments for the lord's family. These powerful Norman lords owned vast tracts of land and property. They would only have lived in the castle for several weeks at a time before moving on to another home with their attendants, leaving a smaller staff to look after the day-to-day affairs of the castle in their absence. (*Jane White*)

Above: The castle's curtain wall may have been whitewashed with lime to make it stand out in the surrounding countryside as a symbol of Norman power. As weapons grew more sophisticated the Normans prevented any building within about 200 metres which could have given attackers places to hide. (*Trevor Scott*)

In one lawn are underground cellars which have now been fenced off. Popularly known as the dungeons, these were in fact probably used for storing supplies. But there was a prison. Written accounts for the years 1265–6 say that two pairs of manacles for the prison cost 6d. (*I.M. Morgan*)

A Norman archer at a re-enactment. It was the Men of Gwent, however, who were the most skilled archers. In his tale, Gerald of Wales says the men of Gwentland (Gwent and Glamorgan) were more experienced in warfare and more skilful with the long bow and arrow than those in any other part of Wales. In one incident, as two Norman men-at-arms rushed across the bridge to shelter in the tower, the Welsh shot at them. Their arrows penetrated the heavy oak door which was almost as thick as four fingers on a man's hand. As a reminder, the arrows were left sticking in the doorway.

The Norman lord William de Braose told Gerald that during an attack on the castle one of his men-at-arms was hit by a Welshman's arrow which pierced his chain-mail, his leather tunic, went through his upper thigh, his saddle, struck his horse and killed it. In another tale, an arrow pierced the thigh of a soldier and went through his saddle to his horse. As he pulled the reins and turned his horse around, another arrow hit him in exactly the same place on the other thigh, skewering him to his horse on both sides. (*I.M. Morgan*)

Opposite: A Welsh Victorian farmhouse kitchen at the museum. (*Abergavenny Museum*)

Abergavenny Castle, early twentieth century. When the Marquess leased the castle to the town in 1881, the grounds were turned into an attraction for visitors. A bandstand, formal gardens and tennis courts were provided and a walkway was built around the top of the castle walls. Huge parties were catered for – an advertisement in an early twentieth-century trade directory says that it could accommodate the feeding of a thousand visitors. (*Abergavenny Museum*)

Most visitors today will pause before the heavy oak door to the museum and gaze at the panoramic view of the Usk river valley. A thousand years ago, Norman lords would also have appreciated that view – for its strategic importance in controlling the river crossing. At that time, a loop of the river would have been closer to the castle. Exhibits at the museum depict the story of the town from prehistoric times to the present day. (*I.M. Morgan*)

Castell Arnallt, the stronghold of Sitsyllt ap Dyfnwal which was destroyed by William de Braose's men in 1175, is situated on private farmland near the River Usk and is about three miles from Abergavenny. All that's left is an oblong mound measuring about 150 metres at its longest and 30 metres at its widest. Preliminary geophysical surveys on the site were undertaken in 1999. It is now under the protection of CADW (Welsh Historic Monuments). (*I.M. Morgan*)

PRIORY

St Mary's Priory, part of the Anglican Church in Wales, has been described as one of the finest churches in Wales. It contains a superb collection of monuments and sculptures said to be the second most important in Britain. The medieval monuments in the Herbert Chapel have been restored in a programme that has been hailed as a magnificent success. But other restoration work continues.

The Lewis Chapel has recently been restored and a fund-raising drive has been started to have the organ rebuilt. The church has bought back the neighbouring medieval tithe barn which has been redeveloped by the St Mary's Priory's Development Trust, whose patron is the Prince of Wales. It will be opened as a visitors' centre, with a 44-seat restaurant, gallery and exhibition area and will house the 20ft Abergavenny Tapestry.

The priory was established at the end of the eleventh century by Hamelin de Ballon to support a prior and twelve monks from the French St Vincent and St Lawrence Abbey in Le Mans. Very little remains of the original structure. The main part of the church dates from the early fourteenth century when the Lord of Abergavenny, John de Hastings, commissioned the building of the tower, the nave, chancel and transepts, and adjoining chapels. The carved fourteenth- and fifteenth-century choir stalls were once separated from the nave by a rood screen. Here the black monks of the Benedictine order assembled several times each day. Aged monks would use the hinged misericord seats to support themselves as they stood during the long services.

The Priory Church's main treasure is the medieval figure of Jesse, which originally depicted the lineage of Jesus Christ from Jesse, the father of King David. These elaborate 'family trees' were popular because few people in medieval times could read and each generation on the tree would have been easily identifiable.

St Mary's and the priory house in the 1960s. After the Reformation most of the original priory buildings were demolished and replaced with a house which was itself demolished in 1952. A new Priory Centre, which stages events and conferences, was officially opened by the Prince of Wales in the year 2000. Some of the original features of the former priory rooms, including walls, windows and a fireplace, have been incorporated into the new centre. (*Romley Marney*)

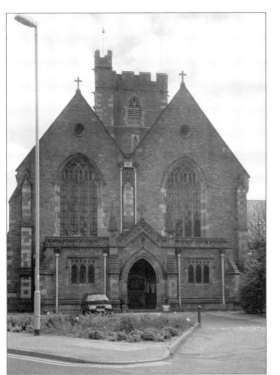

This is the front entrance of St Mary's. Stewards and guides are generally available to help visitors who want to see the church which has been described as the 'Westminster Abbey of Wales'. By the 1980s the condition of the monument was deteriorating as a result of rising damp and a leaking roof. A restoration committee was formed in 1991, funding was sought and found, and experts were then engaged to carry out the intricate work which has since won such wide acclaim. (*I.M. Morgan*)

A very rare view of the church as seen between the restorations of the 1820s and before 1882 when it acquired its familiar double nave. The church has been remodelled at various times. In 1823, the medieval arches that separated the nave from the north aisle were removed, balconies were built and the pulpit was rearranged at the west end of the church. Later, restoration work was carried out to remove the balconies and the pulpit while the nave was almost completely restored and the central arches were erected. (*Abergavenny Museum*)

The magnificently carved Tree of Jesse dates from the fifteenth century, and in its original form it would have shown the lineage of Christ from Jesse, the father of King David. Now only the base remains. The whole figure probably formed the reredos – the ornament placed behind the altar. The Jesse figure lies on his side with his head on a pillow supported by an angel. The Jesse tree is the only one in solid wood to be found in Great Britain and probably the world. Carved from one piece of oak, only the right hand (now missing) would have been added on. It was originally highly coloured and traces of this can still be seen in the folds.

It is regarded as the most significant and finest medieval sculpture to have survived the Reformation and the Civil War and it was the centrepiece of the Image and Idol: Medieval Sculpture exhibition held at London's Tate Britain from September 2001 to March 2002. (*Abergavenny Local History Society*)

This carved wooden figure depicts John de Hastings the younger who rebuilt the priory during the early fourteenth century. He died in 1324 and his effigy now lies on a tomb with panelling remodelled from the original one. His cross-legged posture was a fashion popular in the early fourteenth century, and had nothing to do with involvement with the Crusades. His feet rest on a lion, a symbol of courage and strength. (*Abergavenny Local History Society*)

The Herbert Chapel contains recently restored tombs, mainly of the lords and ladies of Abergavenny. The alabaster tomb of Sir William ap Thomas and his wife Gwladys is one of the most significant. Sir William took the name Herbert and is the ancestor of the Herbert family. When his wife, the daughter of Sir Dafydd Gam, died in 1464, 3,000 knights, nobles and weeping peasants attended her funeral. She was previously the widow of Sir Richard Vaughan who fought with her father at Agincourt. She was known as the 'Star of Gaveuny'. Beyond, the tomb of Lawrence de Hastings depicts a tall, powerful man resting his feet on a bull; the crest of the Hastings family was a bull head. Lawrence, who died in 1348, was the last lord of Abergavenny to be buried at St Mary's. (*S. Morgan*)

The congregation gathered in 1910 outside St Mary's for a memorial service for Edward VII who had died earlier that year. (*Abergavenny Museum*)

Opposite: The view from the north-east side and the outside of the Lewis Chapel. The chapel contains the sixteenth-century tomb of Dr David Lewis who was the eldest son of the vicar. He was the Judge of the High Court of the Admiralty in the reign of Elizabeth I, and was one of the founders and the first principal of Jesus College, Oxford. He was Master of St Catherine's Hospital, London, one of the Masters in Chancery and an MP for Monmouthshire. Dr Lewis, who died in London in 1584, designed the tomb himself. Its decoration shows his links to the Royal Navy. (*Trevor Scott*)

The altar and the medieval choir and sanctuary beyond, showing the eighteenth-century ceiling and the east window. The church is one of the largest parish churches in Wales, measuring 57 metres long. The tower contains a ring of ten bells which were recast in 1948. The four oldest bells date from the fourteenth century, two were added on the restoration of Charles II, two during Queen Victoria's golden jubilee celebrations in 1887 and the remaining two were thanksgiving gifts in 1948. (*Trevor Scott*)

Below: The tithe barn dates back to medieval times. It was burned down in the 1400s during Owain Glyndwr's Welsh war of independence. It was rebuilt with a pitched thatched roof but in the seventeenth century the roof was raised to add an extra floor. Pigeon holes were added and for a time it was used as a stable for the house built on the site of the priory buildings. In recent times it has been a carpet shop and a computer centre, among other things. During the 1960s it was even used for dancing and Saturday night bops. The building has been bought back by the Development Trust and is being restored as a visitors' centre which will have a restaurant and an exhibition area. (*I.M. Morgan*)

Above: On 26 April 2002 the Revd Canon Jeremy Winston blessed the first stitch of the Abergavenny Tapestry, a millennium project celebrating 1,000 years of the town's history. It is expected to take four years to complete at a cost of £20,000. The giant wall tapestry was begun by a group of parishioners led by Sheila Bevan, seated centre, with guest David Davies, Welsh Assembly member, handing the wool to her. After the group was awarded funding, professional advisors were enlisted – the artist Susie Martin, who designed the cartoon with ideas from the group, and Sarah Windrum, the technical advisor. The group has been awarded grants by the Lottery Fund and the Prince's Trust. After completion, the Abergavenny Tapestry will be handed over as a gift for permanent display in the restored tithe barn. (*Sheila Bevan*)

One of the fifty volunteer stitchers at work on the tapestry which will be 6ft high and more than 20ft long. Four hundred shades of colour have been used in moth-proof wool. Visitors to the church can view the work in progress during stitching sessions – and add some stitches themselves. Project organisers say another aim is to help young people acquire skills to aid the preservation of traditional crafts. (*Trevor Scott*)

The parish of St Peter's, Llanwenarth, is now grouped with St Mary's Priory Church and Christchurch but until 1860 it consisted of the two Llanwenarths – Citra on the Abergavenny side of the Usk and Ultra on the far side; they were connected by a rope ferry. The 'far' side now forms part of Govilon. A church, probably dedicated to St Gwaenarth, has existed on this site since about AD 600. The present church dates from 1631, but the font is pre-Norman, probably from an earlier chapel. The ferry stopped operating in 1951 but a post on the north side and a landing ramp on the south bank are still visible. (*Trevor Scott*)

Below: Christchurch in North Street is known as the 'Iron Church' because it was built on an iron framework and then clad in cedar wood. It was built in 1879–80, at a time when Abergavenny was expanding with the coming of the railways. It is now a listed building and a daughter church of St Mary's Priory, serving the western parts of the parish. It was funded through the generosity of the Nevills, the Marquesses of Abergavenny. The church has been restored in recent years. The adjoining schoolroom, opened in 1898, is the centre for a number of community activities. (*Trevor Scott*)

2

Town & Country

No. 14 Nevill Street was extended in about 1780, when it became the Cow Inn (1780–1860s). The distinctive cows' heads were carved at this time. The site of the British Legion nearby once belonged to a hair-bleacher. During the eighteenth century Abergavenny was known for making white periwigs which cost up to 40 guineas. (*Trevor Scott*)

THE GROWTH OF ABERGAVENNY

The site of the Roman fort is now part of the Castle Street car park. In Norman times the town grew up alongside the castle, extending along what is now Castle Street as far as the middle of the present car park. A kink in the wall facing the river meadow marks the western end of the bank and ditch which probably defended the town on that side. In 1241 the town was extended and protected by strong walls. A defensive wall was built with a ditch on the north and probably the east sides to enclose a much larger township. The town was a long D-shaped enclosure with four main gateways. Streets were laid out in a regular pattern. By 1300 only about 7 per cent of residents were Welsh.

The earliest livestock markets in medieval times were held in this area. During attacks by the Welsh, it is thought that cattle were brought in from Castle Meadows through the Tudor gate for safekeeping. Abergavenny was also on a drover's road from West Wales and cattle were rested on Castle Meadows before being taken on to English markets.

Although many buildings seem to be eighteenth- or nineteenth-century in date, some are much older. Nevill Street used to be called Rother Street after a breed of horned cattle, and no. 11, which has a beautiful Adam-style front, is still called Rother House. The pedimented doorway was wide enough to accommodate the women's skirts of the time (*c.* 1750). The first Abergavenny Bank was started in the downstairs room of 5 Nevill Street in 1790 by the Hill family with local backing – Thomas Hill founded Blaenavon Iron Works and his son built the tram road on the Blorenge mountain to his Llanfoist canal.

Nevill Street is one of the architectural delights of Abergavenny. Most of the buildings have Georgian frontages built on Tudor foundations. Built in about 1600, no. 14 was the town house of the Vaughans of Tretower, whose arms can be seen carved on the window sills. As the house adjoins the ancient church of St John's, it is possible that it was connected to it. Thomas Vaughan was the headmaster of the grammar school at the church. Here, too, was found the altar stone from St John's, which is now in Holy Trinity Church. (*Trevor Scott*)

Tudor Street in the late 1950s when demolition work was being carried out. The Kings Arms public house is on the right. During the sixteenth and seventeenth centuries, the street extended beyond the walled town and the Tudor gate. It used to be known as Potidder Street, a corruption of the Welsh 'Porth Tudor' (Tudor Gate). It was once a wealthy part of town where merchants and burgesses built large houses. By the nineteenth century the houses were being sub-divided into tenements for the working classes. (*Maureen Griffiths*)

The same view today with the Kings Arms almost unchanged. When demolition of Tudor Street began, it was discovered that the houses were much older than expected. Early seventeenth-century wall paintings were uncovered and many destroyed. Only a few pieces were salvaged for the museum. (*Trevor Scott*)

A 1775 drawing of the Tudor arch of the West Gate or Tudor Gate before its demolition in the mid-nineteenth century. It was one of four town gates and is said to have been named after a lord of Abergavenny, Jasper Tudor, uncle of Henry VII. The basement of the East gate is thought to have been used as a gaol. (*Abergavenny Museum*)

Below: This fourteenth-century stone arch doorway, originally from the basement at the Tudor Gate, was found in the 1960s and rebuilt behind Abergavenny Museum in the castle grounds. (*Trevor Scott*)

The old Bull Inn in St John's Square with the
Kings Arms opposite and houses in Tudor Street
beyond in the 1950s. The rear of the Bull is where
the post office now stands and a blue plaque
marks the spot. (*Abergavenny Museum*)

Below: Looking across to St John's Square where
the old Bull Inn was situated, *c.* 1990. The King's
Arms, left, is a typical seventeenth-century
coaching inn with a very good Charles II coat of
arms. It was originally jettied and half-timbered,
but the ground floor has been built out beyond the
upper floor. This was one of the last pubs in
Abergavenny to brew its own beer in-house. It was
formerly the home of Delafield's Brewery. The
present building probably dates back to the 1660s.
Inside, there are moulded beams and panelling,
and over the fireplace there is an inscription made
by soldiers billeted there during the Napoleonic
Wars – 'Good quartering forever . . . 1817. 15th
Huzzars'. (*Oswald Jones*)

The residents of Tudor Street, which was demolished in the 1960s, were a closely knit community and every house in the street was represented when 180 former residents and their families held a reunion at Abergavenny Museum on 14 August 1987. Entertainer and gospel singer Bryn Yemm, centre, was in charge of festivities.
(*Abergavenny Museum*)

Tudor Street and the corner of Byefield Lane, left, in the early 1960s. This is now the entrance to a car park. Demolition work started in 1957 and carried on until the 1960s. (*Abergavenny Museum*)

These fireplaces are all that is left of the buildings demolished in Tudor Street near the Tudor Gate surgery. (*Trevor Scott*)

Flannel Street is a comparatively new name for this road which used to be called Butchers Row. It was renamed because of the flannel industry of the seventeenth and eighteenth centuries. When 1 Cross Street was being renovated, a flannel weavers' loom was found there and incorporated into the roof. A blue plaque commemorates the trade. The street used to join up with Castle Street but half of it has been demolished. (*Romley Marney*)

Until the middle of the nineteenth century, the poultry market was held in Chicken Street. The Hen and Chickens public house also gets its name from this. (*Romley Marney*)

Looking over Castle Street to the Blorenge Mountain from the site of the present post office. The smaller pale building with the sign in front is the Old Duke Inn. (*Maureen Griffiths*)

Even modern buildings sometimes get redeveloped. This is the former Burgess building in Flannel Street on 19 December 1989. The site is now a car park. (*Keith W. Jones*)

St John's Square, *c.* 1960, looking towards Abergavenny Town Hall and the site of the yet-to-be-built Burgess building which has since been demolished. The Vine Tree public house is on the left. (*Maureen Griffiths*)

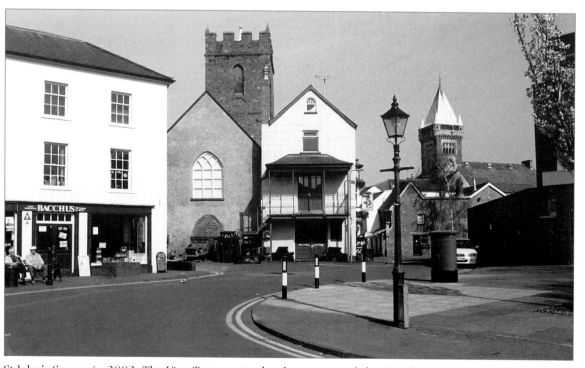

St John's Square in 2003. The Vine Tree, centre, has been renamed the Grasshopper. (*Trevor Scott*)

The former St John's Church is now a freemasons' lodge. In 1542 the disused church became the King Henry VIII grammar school, and the school continued there until 1898. In 1750 the tower was rebuilt, a copy of the original one. In 1898 a new school was built in Pen-y-Pound and the freemasons bought St John's. The lodge was started in about 1813 by prisoners of the Napoleonic War. (*Trevor Scott*)

The ancient piscina basin from St John's Church which has been set in the north wall of the Sanctuary at Holy Trinity Church. It was donated at about the same time as the altar stone (see opposite page). There may have been an earlier church at the St John's site but no evidence has yet been found. St John's church was in a central position in the walled town with the market at its western end. Its graveyard may have stretched across the present High Street to the town wall at the rear of Woolworth's. (*Trevor Scott*)

Holy Trinity Church in Baker Street, in 1957. It was
endowed in 1840 by Miss Rachel Herbert, and is at the
centre of an early Victorian gothic square on the former
Grove Fields. The church forms a compound with the
vicarage, almshouses and the church hall built from the
shell of the former girls' school which burned down.
This was probably the first purpose-built school for girls
in the town. Trinity School closed in 1898. When the
borough council petitioned the philanthropist Andrew
Carnegie to provide a free library for the town, he
agreed as long as the council provided a suitable site. So
it bought the school's old playground and the library
was built in 1905. (*I.M. Morgan*)

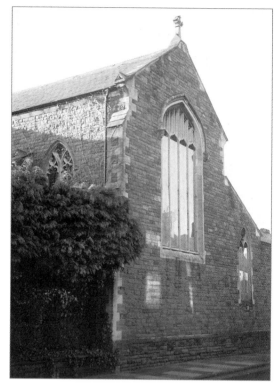

Below: The altar stone was originally part of the ancient
church of St John's, the first parish church of
Abergavenny. It was discovered in 1894 while being
used as a lintel for a fireplace at the old Cow Inn in
Nevill Street. It was found by Illtyd Gardner who later
became vestry clerk and churchwarden, and who, with
his brother Frederick, had taken over the Cow Inn as
solicitors' chambers. They presented it to Holy Trinity
Church and it was reconsecrated on Trinity Sunday
1894. (*Trevor Scott*)

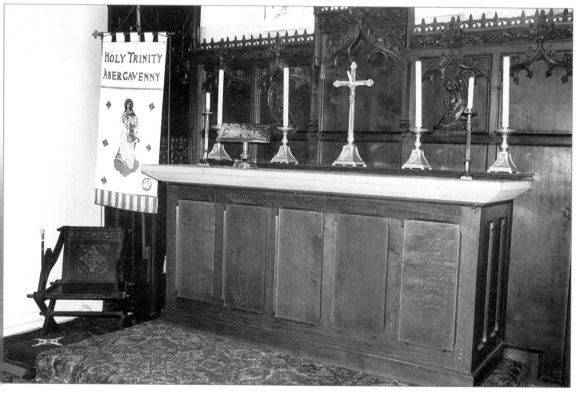

The printing firm Seargeants Bros Ltd had a special place in the heart of many townpeople. Its works' hooter was a familiar sound throughout the town and served as a timekeeper for many. This photograph commemorates the retirement of the chief engineer Mr Tom Myatt, seated with his wife second from right next to Mr Seargeant. In the front row are Jack Goff, Artie Richard and a director, Mr Sidney White. Second row: Ivy Jones, Ada Matthew, Letty Hodges, Nancy Lyons, Elsie Parker, -?-, Phyllis Hearne, Harold Pool, Glyn Williams, Barbara Winters, Doll Davies, Cecil Powell, Gertie Casey and Charlie Gwenlan. (*South Wales Argus*)

The Usk Vale works before it was demolished in about 1990. The site is now the rear of the Cibi shopping Precinct. (*Edna Edwards*)

Frogmore Street Baptist Church has been a landmark building for the west end of the town centre since it was built in 1877. It is pictured here in Edwardian times in the early 1900s. Baptists have a long tradition in Abergavenny and the surrounding area. In 1807 the Abergavenny Baptist Academy was founded in a building in Pen-y-Pound now known as Enon House. The Revd Micah Thomas, who was also the minister of the English Baptists in Abergavenny, ran it for almost thirty years before it was moved to Pontypool. For some time, his congregation met with the Welsh Baptists in Tudor Street, but a new church was built in Frogmore Street in 1815 on part of what is now the Tesco site. The expansion of the town meant a growing congregation so another Frogmore Street church was built. In 1827 a breakaway movement built a new meeting place, the Bethany Baptist Church in Market Street, but in 1988 the two combined to become the Abergavenny Baptist Church. (*Judges*)

Frogmore Street and the Baptist Church with the Rholben and the Sugar Loaf in the distance, in about 1960 before the building of Tesco's. The Trocadero café is on the right next to the post office, which later moved to St John's Square. (*Romley Marney*)

Frogmore Street in about 1988 before the Cibi Walk shopping precinct and its entrance were built. The Cibi Walk shopping precinct which was officially opened in 1989. (*Edna Edwards*)

The same spot in 1998. (*Edna Edwards*)

The Abergavenny and District Co-operative Stores in 1925 at 1 Brecon Road on the corner with St Michael's Road. It was first formed in 1909 and was established in Chicken Street before moving to Brecon Road in 1919. The vehicle appears to be carrying a huge advertising placard. (*Abergavenny Museum*)

Ruther & Son, the family grocers, had premises that extended to Lion Street, above, although the main frontage was at 7 and 8 Frogmore Street. They occupied the premises from about 1910 until 1937. (*Abergavenny Museum*)

In the 1970s, part of the building in High Cross was shored up with unsightly red iron girders which earned the area the nickname 'Red Square', a title the local councils tried hard to discourage. Three tiny shops had to be demolished and an end wall rebuilt. The shops were replaced by display windows for the Abergavenny Tourist Association. A blue plaque displaying the High Cross title has been put up by the History Society. (*Pamela Mason*)

High Cross in 2003 with attractive shop-style display windows and the Abergavenny Mural. At one time, passers-by would reach High Street by climbing a flight of steps from Cross Street. The level of the road and pavement near the Town Hall at the junction of Cross Street and High Street has been substantially raised. Some shops at the top of Cross Street have basements which at one time would have been on the ground floor and the archway by the Kings Head Hotel would have looked more imposing. This area was called High Cross because it was literally a high-level crossroads – the junction of Cross Street/High Street and Market Street/Flannel Street, as opposed to the 'Low Cross' – the Cross Street, Monk Street and Lower Castle Street junction by the Angel Hotel. The theory that High Cross was named because a preaching cross stood there has now been discounted. (*Trevor Scott*)

The Abergavenny Mural by artist Frances Baines has brightened up High Cross to become a well-established tourist attraction. Mrs Baines, of Govilon, was commissioned to carry out the work as a millennium project by Abergavenny Town Council from an idea by former councillor Mrs Edna Edwards. The mural is made up of a scenic view of the town in the year 2000. There are four 'windows into the past' with inset panels each depicting a different period in the town's history. The general view is that seen from the perspective of someone looking across to the town from Llanfoist at the foot of the Blorenge Mountain. The four panels show the first earth and timber castle, a wagon arriving at Tudor Street in about 1600, the road and tram road over the River Usk in the nineteenth century and a steam train at Monmouth Road station in the early twentieth century. (*Trevor Scott*)

This fire insurance plaque in High Street opposite Woolworth's is a replica. The original came from 23 High Street (formerly the gas showroom). It was erected by the Birmingham Fire Insurance Co. in the first half of the nineteenth century. This company provided Abergavenny's first Merryweather (manual) fire engine; it was used in the town until 1921. Plaques of this sort were used as a means of identifying insured buildings before the days of house numbering – and to show which fire brigade was responsible for fighting the fire. (*Abergavenny Local History Society*)

Cross Street from the Angel Hotel looking up to the Town Hall. In 1620 a timber-framed market house was erected in the middle of Cross Street in front of the present Market Hall, which explains the width of the street at this point. By 1794 this was causing so much congestion that the Improvement Commissioners ordered it to be demolished and a new market to be erected on the present site. By the middle of the century it was decided that a covered market was needed and this, with the Town Hall in front, was completed in 1870. (*Trevor Scott*)

Opposite: In the centre of Cross Street is Basil Jones's shop, a traditional grocer's store which had been not been modernised and had been closed down for some time when this photograph was taken in October 1989. The shop was sold off shortly afterwards. The shop's interior was then transported to the Abergavenny Museum and reassembled and is now a major visitors' attraction. (*Keith W. Jones*)

On the opposite side of the road to Basil Jones's shop in Cross Street was newsagent Fred Sadler's, run by brothers Viv and Tom Sadler and pictured in October 1989. It has now been converted into an art shop and gallery. (*Keith W. Jones*)

The changing world. Pictured outside the Angel in about 1903 is this early motor car and horse-drawn trap. The passenger in the trap looks remarkably like Maurice, the groom in the wedding party. (*Abergavenny Museum*)

Edwardian finery on show at the Angel Hotel in Cross Street in 1903 where a family wedding party was hosted by the hotel's owner John Prichard, seated on the right with his wife Helen. The newly married couple are Florence Helen and Maurice. With them standing in the back row are, from left to right: Ralph Brady, his wife Blanche, -?-, Caroline Ann Brady, James Wyndham Prichard and his wife Frances, and Walter Hampson, who is standing behind his wife Mabel Brady Hampson and their son Geoff. Seated on the left are Will, and Mr and Mrs Brady. In front are Barbara Brady, the Sergeant sisters, who are the two little bridesmaids, and their mother.
(*Abergavenny Museum*)

Gunter House, built in about 1600 in Cross Street, stood just outside the medieval South Gate. Here, secret Catholic services were held in the seventeenth century at a time when they were illegal. Two priests, David Lewis and Philip Evans, were hidden here by the owner, Thomas Gunter JP. The two were caught, tried and executed in 1678. David Lewis, son of a headmaster of the grammar school, was canonised in 1970 (*Trevor Scott*)

The Adoration of the Magi, the reredos mural that adorned the altar of the secret chapel at Gunter House, is now on display in the museum. The chapel and mural were only discovered during alterations in 1907, found in the little attic room in the right-hand gable. Attendances at Mass in Gunter House in the seventeenth century were said to be greater than at St Mary's. (*Abergavenny Museum*)

The Tourist Information Centre at Abergavenny
Bus Station, 1998. The building, dating from
1931, was at one time part of the bus depot. The
bus station will be familiar to readers of Harry
Potter because of the Knight Bus which stopped
there to let Madam Marsh get off while Harry was
on his way to London. (*Paddy Wills-Wood*)

The eighteenth-century Tan House, once the centre of Abergavenny's leather industry, which has been
converted and is now part of a housing complex for the retired. It was once a master tanner's home. The
road used to be part of Mill Street, which was once the main thoroughfare from the south before a new
street was constructed in the 1830s. Before that, Mill Street extended up today's Cross Street to the South
Gate. The leather industry and allied trades were among the most important in Abergavenny during the
eighteenth and nineteenth centuries. A tanning industry existed on this site, now in Cross Street, as early as
1691. It was at the far end of town – and downwind – to minimise the nuisance from the smell. Tan pits
and workshops were sited next door behind what is now a garage and car dealer. There was a high demand
for leather for nearby trades such as boot- and shoemaking, saddlery and glove-making. On one site in Cross
Street – where Pinch, the bakers, and Fulgoni, the opticians, are situated – about 150 people were employed
making gloves, boots and shoes. Trade directories show there were many other smaller outlets making
leather goods. The leather trade dwindled towards the end of the nineteenth century, ending between 1884
and 1889. The building of railways in 1854 meant there was competition from new factories in the
Midlands. (*Abergavenny Local History Society*)

MARKETS & FARMING

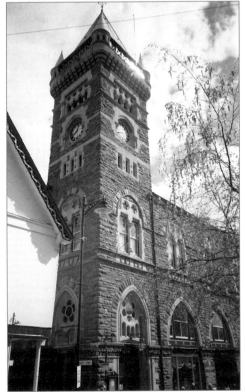

Above: Abergavenny's former market hall was designed by John Nash (before he became famous as George IV's architect and built the Pavilion at Brighton). Built in 1794, it had a classical front, a covered corn market and an open courtyard surrounded by stalls. The old town wall at the back was raised to 14ft to keep out the north wind. The goods sold were corn, flour, meat, fish, poultry, butter, cheese and vegetables; their sale was banned from the streets. This building replaced an earlier hall which lay across the top of Cross Street and caused a great deal of congestion. It was itself replaced in 1870. (*Abergavenny Museum*)

By the middle of the century it was decided that a covered market was needed, and this, with the Town Hall in front, was built in 1870. The clock was donated by Crawshay Bailey, the ironmaster, and its verdigris-capped tower is a landmark. Since those early days, the Tuesday market has extended its range of goods and its size. The Market Hall is used for antique fairs, farmers' markets, craft fairs, auctions, the ice fair and, each September, the Abergavenny Food Festival. (*Trevor Scott*)

Walk down Market Street to see how Abergavenny would have looked around the turn of the sixteenth century. Houses and shops would have been on raised pavements and would have had overhanging first floors supported on wooden jetty posts. These posts were replaced by iron ones at the turn of the nineteenth century when the fronts of the shops were remodelled.

During medieval times, it is likely that townspeople used the street – which probably didn't have a name – as a passage way to gain access to the Cibi brook via a small gate in the town wall so that they could fetch water and do their washing. In times of siege, the gate could have been used to make surprise attacks on the enemy.

In the eighteenth century Market Street was called 'Traitors' Lane' from the legend that during the early 1400s, at the time of the Welsh wars of independence, a sympathiser secretly let in Owain Glyndwr's army through a small gate so that they could launch an attack on the castle and town.

During the twentieth century a number of juggernauts became stuck trying to turn the corner from Cross Street into Market Street. A weight restriction was imposed on vehicles, and the camber of the road was changed to prevent lorries causing any damage to the ancient buildings. (*Trevor Scott*)

Over the centuries Abergavenny has established itself as a major market centre for the surrounding countryside. One of the most important privileges of the medieval town was the right to hold markets. These were controlled by the Norman lords. Today, the traditional Tuesday indoor and outdoor market is one of the major markets in South Wales, drawing visitors from the valleys and tourists from further afield. Other markets are held on a Friday and Saturday. In the twentieth century the indoor market became known as an egg market. Hundreds of cases changed hands each Tuesday and Friday, many of which were sold on in Cardiff and Newport, labelled as 'Abergavenny Eggs'. (*I.M. Morgan*)

Councillor William Horsington, who was three times the mayor, addressing the crowd in the Market Hall in 1958 on Mayor's Sunday. (*Joan Isaac*)

Above: The closure of Cross Street during the 2002 Food Festival led to tables and chairs being set out in the street and visitors enjoyed a continental-type atmosphere. The Food Festival has become a showcase for the best regional Welsh food and wine. More than fifty local and regional specialist growers and manufacturers exhibit each year at the Market Hall and at Abergavenny Castle. Other highlights in 2002 included a banquet served up by top chef Franco Taruschio. Masterclasses are held with tips from chefs and the Welsh Oyster Opening Championships have become a regular event. (*I.M. Morgan*)

The Market Hall interior is decked out with giant streamers by the Crickhowell-based Arts Alive charity. Inside, there's usually a chance to taste such delicacies as Y Fenni cheese (Y Fenni is Welsh for Abergavenny), apple juice and wine made from fruit grown on the slopes of the Sugar Loaf, and Welsh liqueurs produced locally. The Festival Food Bar, cookery demonstrations and children's workshops are hugely successful. Among the celebrity speakers in 2002 were Hugh Fearnley-Whittingstall, Claudia Roden and Monty Don. (*I.M. Morgan*)

Adding a splash of colour to the art workshops organised by Arts Alive in the Abergavenny Castle grounds are these children painting silk. (*I.M. Morgan*)

The Ice Fair at the Market Hall in December only started in millennium year but already it has become a firm favourite with children. A small-scale ice rink is assembled and jugglers, magicians and acrobats provide a programme of entertainment throughout the festival. (*Monmouthshire County Council*)

Abergavenny's livestock market – now earmarked for closure – was opened in 1863 on a former cricket pitch. Before that animals were sold in different streets which derived their names from each trade such as Chicken Street. The notable exception is Lion Street, which was probably named after the Golden Lion pub rather than the king of the jungle. The practice of selling animals in the street led to complaints from townspeople and once the market site was established, sales elsewhere were forbidden. In 1823 a piece of ground in Castle Street belonging to Thomas Gabb was bought and turned into a sheep market. Castle Street was also used for exhibiting stud horses. The south-west side of Lion Street, Lower Monk Street and Ross Road were used to sell cattle. Nevill Street was previously called Rother Street (rother means horned cattle), which suggests that it was used for selling cows. (*I.M. Morgan*)

Mr Tom Watkins, of Newhouse Farm, Llandewi Rhydderch, who won the Welsh Sheepdog Championship in 1966 with his dog Floss. Mr Watkins, seen here with another of his sheepdogs, competed in trials held at Chester Racecourse. His family have a long tradition of farming in the area. (*Glyn Harris*)

The committee and guests at the annual Abergavenny Horse Show in 1956 at Bailey Park. The horse show led to the formation of the Abergavenny and Border Counties Agricultural Show. Among the civic dignitaries is Councillor Reg Silverthorne, Mayor of Abergavenny, seated third from left. (*Maureen Griffiths*)

The President of the 1989 Abergavenny and Border Counties Show, Richard Merton Jones, centre, is pictured with several past presidents: Mr Herbert Spencer, Mr and Mrs Ralph Godfrey, show chairman Mr Brian Foster, Mr R.J. Lewis and Mrs Merton Jones, right. The Border Counties Show, held at Llanwenarth ended in 1996 after nearly 150 years of tradition. It had started through general horse trading, which progressed to the Horse Show at Bailey Park, which in turn became the Border Counties Agricultural Show. The main reasons for ending the show were falling attendances, a decline in sponsorship and the participation of the community, and more stringent health and safety checks, which meant rising costs. (*Oswald Jones*)

The Fatstock Show at Abergavenny Market with the Mayor of Abergavenny, Councillor Reg Silverthorne, in 1956. (*Maureen Griffiths*)

Gwyn Jones of Llangibby is presented with the Oakden Toby Fisher Memorial Cup for the supreme champion in the cattle classes at the 1989 Abergavenny and Border Counties Show by the show's president Richard Merton Jones. (*Oswald Jones*)

The South Wales Shire Horse Society was formed in 1983 after smaller shows and sales were held in Brecon in 1980 and then Builth Wells. Its first show in Abergavenny was held in 1983 at Bailey Park and it is now a qualifying event for the Shire Horse of the Year Championship. This photograph was taken in about 1985. (*South Wales Argus*)

Joyce Morgan of Trellech receives the Stallion Cup with her horse Decoy Williams at the South Wales Shire Horse Society show, *c.* 1985. Exhibitors come from as far afield as the West Country, Lancashire, Cheshire, North Wales, West Wales, the Midlands and South Wales. Members of the Musketeers, Pandy & Monnowside Ploughing Society and the Young Farmers' Clubs are among the volunteers who help out each year.
(*South Wales Argus*)

Taking a well-earned break during hay making at Red Barn Farm at the turn of the nineteenth century. The farm used to be part of the estate of the Marquess of Abergavenny and was sold in 1916. The barn had a capital 'A' built into it – similar to other properties in town – which indicated that it was part of his estate. (*Abergavenny Museum*)

The Pandy & Monnowside Ploughing Society has been in existence since 1867 and is one of the oldest in South Wales. It is a family-oriented society including many successive generations of the same family among its members. Pictured here is a competitor at the annual show at Pandy ploughing a furrow in the shadow of the Black Mountains. (*Abergavenny Museum*)

A ploughing match in the early 1990s in the Herefordshire countryside where many members of the Pandy & Monnowside Ploughing Society and the Welsh Ploughing Association compete. (*Mrs Angela Vaughan*)

Winners of the annual Llantilio Pertholey Village Produce Association show in 1989. The VPA started in 1956 and now has about ninety members who meet in the Mardy Community Centre. Members' competitions and the annual show are well supported with an encouraging level of entries from children in three age groups. (*Oswald Jones*)

OPEN SPACES & PARKLAND

The Sugar Loaf Mountain (Mynydd Pen-y-Fal) and its foothills, the Deri, Rholben and Llanwenarth Breast, are among the seven hills that surround Abergavenny. The others are the Blorenge, the Skirrid Fawr (also known as the Holy Mountain) and the Skirrid Fach or Little Skirrid. The distinctive peak of the Sugar Loaf – it resembles the cone-shaped blocks of sugar which were once imported into the country – draws thousands of hikers who want to climb its summit for the glorious views as far as the Severn estuary. More casual ramblers might be pleased to know that there is a car park a little way up. Legend has it that the fissures in the Skirrid (Ysgyryd Fawr) which is 1,595ft high, were caused by an earthquake at the time of the Crucifixion or that Noah caused them when he passed over in the Flood. But they were in fact caused by geological landslips. It bears the remains of an Iron Age fort and also a few stones of the doorway from St Michael's, a chapel used by Roman Catholics during times of persecution in 1680.

The slopes of the Sugar Loaf were once prime hunting grounds. There is a well-preserved medieval deer park, with much of its boundary bank (up to 2 metres high), a ditch and some of the boundary wall still in place. The ridge of the boundary bank can be seen on the skyline and runs round the crest of the Afon Cibi valley. The deer park was owned by either the priory or the lords of Abergavenny. It is a grade II listed site and the Sugar Loaf woodlands are a site of special scientific interest. (*Trevor Scott*)

A paraglider's view of Abergavenny and surrounding villages and the unmistakable shape of the Skirrid Fawr or Holy Mountain seen after take-off from the Blorenge Mountain. (*Christopher White*)

The bandstand at Bailey Park which was used by the Abergavenny Borough Band. The iron framework used to construct the bandstand was salvaged from the Abergavenny Cattle Market, where it was known as the 'Round House' – it contained shops and a urinal which were demolished. The park is a popular venue for everything from civic events to agricultural fairs and sports to carnivals. There are now plans to upgrade the park as a heritage site. The land was leased by Crawshay Bailey II, an ironmaster, on a 21-year lease. He had it laid out as a park and after his death in 1884 the Improvement Commissioners bought the freehold for £5,000 after launching a fund to which Crawshay Bailey's family donated money. (*Trevor Scott*)

3

Hospitals

Since the middle of the nineteenth century Abergavenny has been a hospital town. Pen-y-Fal Hospital (1851–1996) was first built as a joint counties' asylum and at its peak had more than 1,000 patients. Before then, the workhouse (founded in 1839) dealt with some of those who were poor, infirm or needed medical help. Land to build the Abergavenny Workhouse was bought from a Mr Benoni Peach in 1838. The building in what is now Union Road replaced an earlier workhouse in Mill Street and then Castle Street. It is now the base for a number of businesses. (*Trevor Scott*)

ABERGAVENNY UNION.

NOTICE IS HEREBY GIVEN,

THAT ALL

TRAMPS

AND

VAGRANTS

Seeking Relief within this Union,

MUST APPLY AT

The Police Station, Abergavenny

By Order of the Board of Guardians,

WM. F. BATT, Clerk.

PRINTED BY J. S. MEREDITH, STAMP OFFICE, ABERGAVENNY.

Entry to the workhouse was strictly controlled, as can be seen from this notice. (*Gwent Record Office*)

The workhouse bell used to be housed in a tower in the centre of the workhouse complex. It controlled the lives of the inmates and was a way of knowing the time in the days of few clocks and even fewer watches. The tolling of the bell would summon inmates to rise, to meals and to bed. Now the bell is at Abergavenny Museum. (*Trevor Scott*)

ABERGAVENNY UNION.

DIETARY

FOR

ABLE-BODIED MEN, WOMEN & OTHERS.

| | BREAKFAST. | | DINNER. | | | | SUPPER. | | |
	BREAD. OUNCES.	GRUEL. PINTS.	COOKED MEAT OUNCES.	SOUP. PINTS.	POTATOES. POUND.	Suet or Rice PUDDING OUNCES.	BREAD. OUNCES.	CHEESE OUNCES.	BROTH. PINTS.
SUNDAY									
Men	6	1½	4	-	1	-	6	-	1
Women . .	5	1½	3	-	1	-	5	-	1
MONDAY									
Men	6	1½	-	1½	½	-	6	1½	-
Women . .	5	1½	-	1½	½	-	5	1½	-
TUESDAY									
Men	6	1½	-	-	-	14	6	1½	-
Women . .	5	1½	-	-	-	12	5	1½	-
WEDNESDAY									
Men	6	1½	4	-	1	-	6	-	I
Women . .	5	1½	3	-	1	-	5	-	I
THURSDAY									
Men	6	1½	-	1½	½	-	6	1½	-
Women . .	5	1½	-	1½	½	-	5	1½	-
FRIDAY									
Men	6	1½	-	-	-	14	6	1½	-
Women . .	5	1½	-	-	-	12	5	1½	-
SATURDAY									
Men	6	1½	-	1½	½	-	6	1½	-
Women . .	5	1½	-	1½	½	-	5	1½	-

And we do hereby empower the Guardians of the Poor of the said Union to allow to each infirm person resident in the Workhouse, a sufficient quantity of Tea, properly sweetened, with an allowance of Butter, not exceeding five ounces per week, in lieu of the Gruel for Breakfast.

And we do hereby further order and direct, that Children under the Age of Nine Years, resident in the Workhouse, shall be fed, dieted, and maintained with such food and in such manner as the said Guardians shall direct; and that Children above the Age of Nine Years, and under the Age of Sixteen Years, shall be allowed the same quantities as are prescribed in the above Table for Women.

And we do also order and direct, that the Sick Paupers resident in the said Workhouse shall be fed, dieted, and maintained in such manner as the Medical Officer for the Workhouse shall direct.

And we do hereby further order and direct, that the Master or Masters of the Workhouse or Workhouses of the said Union, shall cause two or more Copies of this our Order, legibly written, or printed in a large type, to be hung up in the most Public Places of such Workhouse, and to renew the same from time to time, so that it always be kept fair and legible.

Given under our Hands and Seal of Office, this Fifth day of March, in the Year One Thousand Eight Hundred and Forty-Four.

(Signed) { GEO. NICHOLLS. G. C. LEWIS. EDMOND W. HEAD.

[Printed by C. Denton, Stamp Office, Abergavenny.

Workhouse food was strictly regulated – conditions were harsh so that people were deterred from applying and being a burden on the parish. If they could not afford to pay the *2d* per night, inmates earned their keep by manual labour. (*Gwent Record Office*)

Pen-y-Fal Hospital, designed by Fulljames and Waller of Gloucester, was originally built as a lunatic asylum to serve Monmouthshire, Herefordshire and Brecon & Radnorshire. It opened in December 1851 and closed in 1996. It was an example of an architectural style which became known as Gothic Rationalism. At its peak it had more than 1,000 patients and was like a self-contained village with its own farm and employing its own craftsmen. The grade II listed hospital building and the site have been developed by Redrow Homes and converted into luxury apartments and houses. (*Trevor Scott*)

The new housing development at the former Pen-y-Fal Hospital, now called Parc Pen-y-Fal. (*I.M. Morgan*)

A male nurse, called an attendant,
in Edwardian days. (*David Bowen*)

A nurse at Pen-y-Fal Hospital in Edwardian
days. (*David Bowen*)

Nurses at Pen-y-Fal Hospital in the early twentieth century. (*David Bowen*)

Tutor David Bowen with student nurses at Pen-y-Fal Hospital during the 1970s. (*David Bowen*)

Drum majorettes getting ready to perform at a fête in the 1970s. The fêtes and sports days at Pen-y-Fal Hospital were well supported. The fête grew out of the annual 'picnic day', enjoyed by both patients and staff. (*David Bowen*)

The former Pen-y-Fal chapel dates from the 1880s and has been designated a listed building. (*Keith W. Jones*)

Nevill Hall Hospital was opened in 1969 and has 436 beds covering a range of specialist services. The hospital is a designated major trauma centre with an accident and emergency department and is staffed by more than 1,800 employees. There is a Post Graduate Medical Centre, opened in 2002, which hosts training in a range of specialties as well as providing teaching for doctors in training. The hospital also has a millennium garden. (*Trevor Scott*)

In the nineteenth century Nevill Hall was called The Brooks before it was bought by the Marquess of Abergavenny. The old Nevill Hall Hospital was first used as a convalescent home by the Blaina Hospital Board who acquired it in 1920. The site was redeveloped as a general hospital for northern Gwent and southern Powys in the 1960s. (*Trevor Scott*)

More than £250,000 has been raised by The Women's Royal Voluntary Service through their shop at Nevill Hall Hospital since 1975. About forty-five members work in shifts to staff the outlet which opened in 2001, replacing the previous 'cubby-hole'-style shop. (*Dr Donald Fry*)

Since its formation in 1955, the League of Nevill Hall Friends has raised more than £500,000, an impressive achievement for a band of dedicated volunteers who staff the coffee bar on a two-hour shift system. Pictured here at a presentation in 1992 are hospital staff and Friends' committee, including the then president, Mrs M. Furzey, and the chairman, Miss Verena Russell-Clarke. Over the years, the Friends have bought medical equipment, bed screens, lighting systems, TV sets and chairs. So much has been handed over that a board in the main hospital concourse lists all the major donations over the years. (*Malcolm Lewis*)

The old-style canteen has been superseded by a bright new coffee bar in the out-patients' department. Volunteers also take a library trolley around the wards and one day a week some take turns in staffing the welcome desk, ready to give directions or get wheelchairs for visitors. In the coffee bar are Ethel Dodd, Myrtle Campbell, Florence Thomas and David Thomas. (*Peter Campbell*)

Abergavenny has its own radio station in Nevill Hall Sound. Jane Hamilton Parker, known as 'Mrs P', was a founder member of the radio station, originally called Radio PYF, which started in 1979. She retired a few years ago. Nevill Hall Sound broadcasts for twenty-four hours, seven days a week, offering a mix of music, features, interviews, Welsh language programmes and outside broadcasts. During the day, a team of around twenty presenters, producers and contributors broadcast live, and an automated service takes over at night. Volunteers range from 15-year-old Gareth Sweeney to retired storekeeper Glyn Parry. (*Oswold Jones*)

Pictured is Steve Powell, Nevill Hall Sound director of programmes, who also works for BBC Radio Wales. Since 2002 family and friends living within a five-mile radius of Nevill Hall Hospital can hear their requests being played out live on air for their loved ones by tuning into 1287 AM on the medium wave band. Around £34,000 was raised, mainly through grants, to refurbish the Old Workhouse studios in Hatherleigh Place and to invest in new transmission equipment. (*Steve Powell*)

Victoria Cottage Hospital was opened in 1902 and named as a memorial to Queen Victoria. It was enlarged and a maternity unit (opened by the late Queen Mother, then Duchess of York) was also based there until 1973. The site has been turned into housing for the elderly. The hospital had its origins in the town's dispensary in Castle Street which was funded by wealthier townsfolk. (*Pam Mason*)

Dr Griffiths and matron planting a tree at Victoria Cottage Hospital. (*Romley Marney*)

Maindiff Court mansion before it was demolished and the site redeveloped as a hospital providing mental health care facilities. The house's previous occupants were the Crawshay Bailey family in the 1870s. It had been used as an annexe to the Pen-y-Fal Hospital from about 1925. The new hospital was opened in 1938 and used by the military during the Second World War. One of its most noted patients was Rudolf Hess, deputy to Adolf Hitler. Rudolf Hess flew to Britain on 10 May 1941. He was hoping to meet the Duke of Hamilton in Scotland but ended up as a prisoner of war. He arrived in Abergavenny in June 1942 and stayed in the town until autumn 1945. He was kept at Maindiff Court where two rooms were converted for his use. He had thirty guards and six Royal Army Medical Corps personnel. Local people, who called him the Kaiser of Abergavenny, kept his stay a close secret, although many saw him as he was escorted on walks in the area. One of his favourite walks was to White Castle and he used to wave at local children. Maindiff Court today comprises four wards, a day hospital and an ECT Department which lie within beautifully kept grounds. The remains of the original balustrade can be seen leading down to the day hospital. (*Abergavenny Museum*)

4

Language, Culture & Entertainment

Augusta Waddington was born in Llanover of English parents in 1802; she was the heiress of the Llanover estate. In 1823 she married Benjamin Hall (later Lord Llanover) uniting the Llanover and Abercarn estates. Hall was a prominent MP. He was Chief Commissioner of Works when Big Ben was commissioned and it was named after him. By 1834 Lady Llanover had learnt Welsh and she won a prize in the Cardiff Eisteddfod for an essay on the Welsh language under the *nom de plume* 'Gwenynen Gwent' (the Bee of Gwent). Her servants were given Welsh names and were required to wear traditional Welsh costume and to speak Welsh. Llanover Court was renowned for its patronage of harpists and bards. She abhorred alcohol and bought up all the public houses in order to close them down or turn them into tea-rooms. (*Llandovery College*)

THE WELSH TRADITION

Abergavenny and the county of Monmouthshire have a strong Welsh tradition with extensive links to Welsh language and culture. Welsh was the predominant language in the Abergavenny area until the middle of the nineteenth century, and it dominated people's religious and social lives.

During the nineteenth century Abergavenny held eisteddfodau which played an important part in the development of the National Eisteddfod of Wales. In the late 1830s, Lady Llanover, known for promoting Welsh language and culture, especially the national costume and the triple harp, became active in the Welsh society, Cymreigyddion Y Fenni. Between 1834 and 1853, the town's eisteddfod became the largest in Wales, attracting visitors from as far afield as Sardinia and Denmark, and a hall was even built to stage the event.

The great cultural tradition of the town eisteddfod has now been revived. The year 2002 saw the first Abergavenny Eisteddfod since 1938 and the response to the schools-only event was so great that the 2003 event was extended to include classes for adults. The last National Eisteddfod in Abergavenny was held in 1913. Organisers hope that the twenty-first century revival will strengthen their case to hold the National Eisteddfod in the town as close as possible to the centenary year.

Children from Llanover School dance the Llanover reel on St David's Day, 1980. This dance was promoted to great effect by Lady Llanover. (*Abergavenny Museum*)

Members of the Welsh society Cymreigyddion Y Fenni during the 1930s. (*Abergavenny Museum*)

Musicians including Theresa Munkley (second from left) with the triple harps favoured by Lady Llanover, 1909. The women are in Llanover costume. (*Abergavenny Museum*)

The ladies of Llanover in the Pageant of Gwent, part of the National Eisteddfod held in Abergavenny in 1913. (*H. Shackleton*)

Children from Our Lady and St Michael's School in costume. (*Our Lady and St Michael's School*)

Children from Llanover Primary and Harold Road schools with guests at the unveiling of the bardic stones in March 2002. The bardic circle of sixteen Gorsedd stones and a central plinth were a legacy from the 1913 National Eisteddfod at Abergavenny and were once the focal point of ceremonies. They lay almost forgotten in an overgrown field on the edge of town near Monmouth Road until a campaign by Mrs Edwards and Mr Robin Tod led to their being moved to a more prominent site in Swan Meadows next to the bus station and tourist office. (*South Wales Argus*)

TWIN TOWNS

Abergavenny's links with other European countries have led to twinning arrangements with three towns – Oestringen in Germany, Beaupreau in France and Sarno in Italy – with delegations usually paying a visit every other year, and streets being named in honour of the twin towns. All three towns were invited to the 2003 Abergavenny Food Festival to give the event even more of an international flavour.

The year 2003 sees the thirty-fifth anniversary of the first twinning arrangement with Oestringen in the German county of Karlsruhe. Both towns were linked through industry. A number of Abergavenny people worked at the ICI Fibres plant, later called DuPont, in Mamhilad. The firm also had a works in Oestringen to which some Abergavenny people were seconded.

Approaches about twinning were first made in 1963 and arrangements were finalised in 1968. Since then, there have been regular exchanges between schools – especially the music and sports departments of King Henry School and Real Schule Gymnasium – and cultural organisations. It is estimated that over 3,000 children have exchanged visits between the two towns. The twinning association, chaired by Councillor Andre Arkell, was formed in 1974 and liaises closely with groups interested in exchange visits.

The links with Beaupreau began in 1988 when a French teacher visited Abergavenny with a party of children. She was so impressed by the town, its countryside and the people that when she returned home she asked the town council to consider linking the towns. They agreed and arrangements were confirmed in 1988 at Abergavenny and 1989 at Beaupreau. The French town, with around 8,000 inhabitants, is situated in an agricultural district south of the Loire river. The town has the smallest racecourse in France – and the biggest one-day fair, the 'Foire de la Petite Angevine'. The main industries are shoe manufacture, exporting trainers and other sports shoes, and wine-making. The area is famous for its vineyards, producing the rosé wine Cabernet d'Anjou and the Côtes du Lyon, a rich golden dessert wine. Every ten years Beaupreau invites representatives from its twin towns in Germany and Wales to a three-day Europiad of swimming, football, gymnastics, athletics, cycling and judo. The last one was held in 2001.

Little did anyone realise that tragedy would strike Abergavenny's Italian twin town days after arrangements had been finalised. Abergavenny was linked in 1997 with Sarno, in the Campania region, fulfilling an ambition for Italian-born Tina Meredith, who had worked for many years to forge a closer bond between her adopted town and her homeland. An Italian delegation visited Wales that September for the official ceremony and an Abergavenny party made the return trip to Sarno, which lies about 20 miles from Naples, the following April.

Only a few days later in May 1998, the southern Italian town was devastated by a mudslide which killed more than 130 people. The Abergavenny twinning committee, with Mrs Meredith as chairwoman, raised funds and bought a four-wheel drive vehicle to help. Since then, Sarno has slowly made a recovery and it is expected that return visits will soon be renewed. Mrs Meredith, who was born in the Naples area, has now retired and Jane White has taken over as chairwoman.

The silver anniversary celebrations of the twinning arrangements between Abergavenny and Oestringen. On the left is the Mayor of Abergavenny, Councillor Alan Breeze, his wife Thelma and Councillor Andre Arkell. The Oestringen Burgermeister Erich Bamberger, who retired in 2003, is fourth from the right. (*Roland Bath*)

Celebrating the fifteenth anniversary of the links with the French town of Beaupreau are some of the members of the twinning association committee in 2003. (*Abergavenny–Beaupreau Twinning Association*)

Councillor Graham Preece, Mayor of Abergavenny, centre left, with the Mayor of Sarno during a visit to Harold Road School in 1997. (*Jane White*)

ENTERTAINMENT

Members of Gwent Young People's Theatre in the Golden Masque of Agamemnon at Abergavenny Castle, 2001. GYPT is based at the Drama Centre in the former King Henry School building in Pen-y-Pound where facilities include the Melville Theatre. It is run by Gwent Theatre with funding from Monmouthshire County Council and the WEA South Wales. The youth theatre, whose patron is the actor Victor Spinetti, has provided access to the performing arts for thousands of young people some of whom, like actress Caroline Sheen, have gone on to make the stage their career. (*Jenny Barnes*)

Halt! Who goes there! Actors from Gwent Theatre, which provides a theatre-in-education service for schools throughout Greater Gwent and Caerphilly, in their production of The Tinderbox. The company also manages GYPT and the Melville Theatre, which has a regular programme of performances and films. (*Jenny Barnes*)

The Gwent Bach Society in the mid-1980s. The society was formed after the bicentenary of Johann Sebastian Bach's death in 1950. The commemorative concerts, especially those held in Bath Abbey, inspired a group of Abergavenny musicians to come together to sing and play Bach's music. The prime movers in the society's formation were Dr Lloyd Davies and his eldest brother, Dr Trevor Davies. They were joined by Dr Reginald Lodge, Leo Harrington, Frank Salter (the first conductor), Rae Edwards and violinist Dorothy Wood. The society has held a number of J.S. Bach festivals and has had Pablo Casals, Paul Tortelier and Dr George Guest as presidents. (*Gwent Bach Society*)

The Abergavenny Operatic and Dramatic Society's production of *Oklahoma* in 1963. (*Pat & Margaret Martin*)

. . . and the same show in 2003. (*Malcolm Lewis*)

Back row, left to right: Patrick Martin, Major Bill Garret, Reg Jones and John Jenkins. Front row: Ted Western, Dilys Sayce, Rene Martin and Tom Richards in the Abergavenny Operatic and Dramatic Society's 1964 production of *Kismet*.

Abergavenny Operatic and Dramatic Society has a long and proud history. Known at its formation as the Abergavenny Operatic Society, its first production in 1911 was *A Nautical Knot*. Among the cast were L. Evans, C. Marsh, J. Morgan and W. Shackleton.

The society has had a continuous run of productions since its foundation, with the exception of breaks during the world wars. After 1947 a number of people came to the fore, including Reg Williams, Dilys Sayce, Betty Rice, Ron Ball, Tom Richards, Harry Giles, Cyril Walters and Archie Leonard. Some years later they were joined by Maureen McCormack, Geoff Allen, Percy Fraser and Edith Northway. In 1950 Major A. Bull became president, an association with the society which lasted twenty-four years.

The society has continued with two shows a year and the junior section goes from strength to strength. Among the society's many highlights was the 1990 production of *Annie* with a cast of juniors and seniors. At the same time, Abergavenny was celebrating its 900th anniversary, and the Borough Theatre was being refurbished.

One former member, Oliver Thornton, now known as Rhoe Thornton, has starred in a German production of *Starlight Express* and in *Chicago* at the Adelphi Theatre, London.
(*Pat & Margaret Martin*)

Showing a leg. Left to right: Major Bill Garret, Patrick Martin, Julian Clark and Derrick Watkins in the Abergavenny Operatic and Dramatic Society's production of *White Horse Inn* in 1967. (*Romley Marney*)

The Gwent Singers, with conductor Derrick Watkins, on the pathway leading up to Abergavenny Museum during the production of a video made with local entertainer Bryn Yemm in the late 1980s. Mr Watkins formed the choir in 1972. They were invited to perform with actress Sarah Churchill. Since then the Abergavenny-based mixed choir, who practise at the Angel Hotel, have raised more than £400,000 for charity. (*Maureen Griffiths*)

Abergavenny drummer John Gibbon, marking twenty-five years in the music business in 2001, at the popular 'Music in the Park' series of concerts run each year at Linda Vista Gardens where the audience can bring a picnic during the Abergavenny Arts Festival. The festival has been going since 1993, emerging from the successful Abergavenny 900 celebrations and the Heritage Festival. Its small hard-working committee is supported by the many organisations, societies and venues in the town. (*South Wales Argus*)

Abergavenny Light Opera's *Mikado* from 1967. The lead baritone singer was Carl Marshall, who is now a life member of the Abergavenny Light Opera Company. He retired from the stage after thirty-seven years. The company was formed in 1966 as an offshoot of the town's Amateur Operatic and Dramatic Society. (*Carl Marshall*)

Abergavenny Light Opera's show *The Mikado* in 1999. *Call me Madam* was the company's 2003 production and their 2004 show is to be Ivor Novello's *Dancing Years*. (*Malcolm Lewis*)

In the late 1980s and early 1990s an annual medieval fair was held in the town. Nevill Street was closed off and turned into a market-place. Here are some of the visitors to the 1989 event. (*Oswald Jones*)

Abergavenny Pantomime Company was formed in 1932 and is thought to be the oldest amateur pantomime company in Wales. It was originally called the Holy Trinity Pantomime Company. (*Malcolm Lewis*)

Abergavenny Borough Band at the 1972 national championships held in Camden Town Hall, London. Abergavenny Borough Band members have won a loyal following whether they are heading a town parade appearing at the Borough Theatre or playing a concert in Linda Vista Gardens on a summer afternoon. But in addition to winning the hearts of townspeople they have notched up an impressive array of championship awards and trophies in competitions. Their headquarters is a former chapel in Prospect Road which has been 'home' since 1965. The band bought the building in 1971, then extended it – and soundproofed it.

The band was formed some time in the nineteenth century. The exact date is uncertain because the wooden bandroom – built by the unemployed during the Depression of the 1920s and 1930s – in the Fairfield burned down in 1962, destroying many instruments, a fine library and all the band's archives. However, there is evidence that the band existed before 1884 and it is thought to have started many years before that.

After the fire, the future of the band hung in the balance but the chairman, the late Bill Parry, with other dedicated people, took on the task of replacing the instruments through fund-raising. Mr Parry also pieced together the band's history from his own memories and other archives.

The Abergavenny Silver Band, as it was once called, acquired the right to be called the borough band in 1906 following the visit of the Boer War commander-in-chief, Earl Roberts VC. The band headed the civic parade and from then was also allowed to use the borough coat of arms. For about four years after the First World War, it was also the 3rd Monmouthshire Battalion Regiment Band. The word 'Silver' was dropped from the band's title about this time.

For a time the band had an unsettled existence, rehearsing in a room which was a public mortuary, the Fairfield and other places, including the Old Volunteers Hall where boxing matches were held – the band used to rehearse in the boxing ring on Sunday mornings. Then it moved back to the building in the Fairfield which later burned down.

The band kept going during the Second World War, with the help of servicemen who were stationed in the town. Since then it has gone from strength to strength. The year 2002 saw the retirement of musical director Eric Powell who first joined in 1963 as an instructor for the youth section. Three years later he became the bandmaster for the Borough Band. During his leadership, the band won successive promotion from the fourth section to reach class 'A' competition status. Among the band's proudest moments was its appearance at the Royal Albert Hall in the national brass band finals in 1979. Mr Powell has been succeeded by Lyndon Price. (*Abergavenny Borough Band*)

ergavenny Borough Band with its tally of seven trophies in 1991. (*Abergavenny Borough Band*)

e Youth Band after their success in Section Two at the Gwent Youth Brass Band Festival in 2003 with
iductor Lyndon Price. The festival was held at Cross Keys College. The youth section was founded in
out 1952 with some well-worn instruments donated by the defunct Pen-y-Fal Hospital Band.
nmouthshire County Council helped the band to get some new instruments and music classes for
ingsters were soon organised. In 1963 Eric Powell, who retired in 2002, took over as conductor. The
ith Band started to compete in county contests in 1972, and since then the youngsters have built up a
ining tradition of their own. (*R &P Photographic Service*)

Kings of the road. The float from the Abergavenny Chamber of Trade won first prize in the best overall and most original entry in the 1989 carnival with the entry 'Taff McNaff and the Road Menders', an iron comment on the number of roadworks around the town that summer. (*Oswald Jones*)

The Hen and Chickens pub float won the prize for the best commercial entry in the 1989 summer carnival. In all there were eleven floats and twenty walking entries. (*Oswald Jones*)

Members of Abergavenny Chamber of Trade and their friends have a chance to let their hair down at their annual Picnic in the Park at Tredilion Park in 2002. (*Abergavenny Chamber of Trade*)

Aloha! Hula-hula dancing at the Picnic in the Park to the sound of a Beach Boys tribute band in 2002. (*Abergavenny Chamber of Trade*)

One of the most popular social clubs after the Second World War was the Methodist Youth Club. Here are some of the young men at one of their social events in August 1947. (*Pamela Mason*)

The girls of the Methodist Youth Club take their turn in front of the camera in 1947. (*Pamela Mason*)

CHURCHES

The Roman Catholic Church of Our Lady and St Michael in Pen-y-Pound was completed in 1860 and is thought to be the work of Benjamin Joseph Bucknall, who was born in Rodborough in 1833. Earlier Roman Catholic churches were located in Frogmore Street (it is now a printers) and Lewis Lane. Our Lady and St Michael has a memorial to St David Lewis who was executed after being arrested for saying Mass in Gunter House in 1678. (*Trevor Scott*)

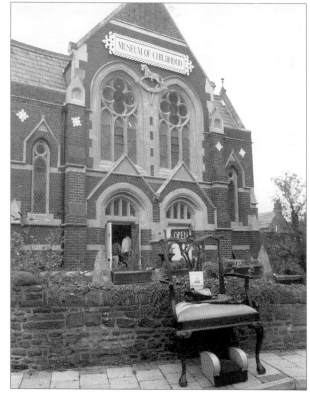

The Museum of Childhood, Market Street, 1992. The museum was located in the former Bethany Baptist Church. This is now a furniture recycling centre. (*Keith W. Jones*)

Llanwenarth Baptist Church is the oldest Baptist fellowship now existing in Wales. It is thought to have been founded in 1652 and an extensive programme of 350th anniversary celebrations was held during 2002, including a hymn-singing festival pictured here on 29 March. The lighting of the cross outside the church marked the beginning of the year with monthly events being held, including a concert, a chapel history exhibition (at which the anniversary wall-hanging was unveiled) and the publication of a special book. (*Frances Baines*)

The Methodist Church in Castle Street was first used in 1829. The first Methodist congregation in the town was formed in 1804 and the following year it bought 22 Tudor Street and adapted it. It then moved to Castle Street. The congregation's original home in Tudor Street was taken over by the Abergavenny Cymreigyddion Society who had a large hall built for their eisteddfodau. The building then became a pub, was converted to a drill hall and then a pub again, which became known as the Volunteer Inn. (*Trevor Scott*)

The Castle Street United Reformed Church. The Abergavenny Independents were described in 1877 as the oldest dissenting body in the county. They had been worshipping since at least 1688 in their first meeting house which stood on the corner of Monk Street and Cross Street on a site now occupied by the Great George. In 1690 they moved to Castle Street until the congregation increased so much that in 1792 they moved to a building further along the road. (*Trevor Scott*)

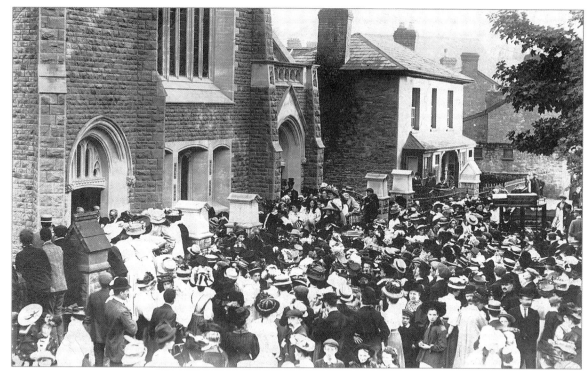

The Whitfield Presbyterian Church in Pen-y-Pound was opened in 1908. In 1871 part of the congregation of the Castle Street Independent Chapel broke away and built a Presbyterian Chapel in Frogmore Street before moving to Pen-y-Pound. (*Abergavenny Museum*)

The former Pavilion cinema and bingo hall in Monk Street is now occupied by the Family Church, which moved from Castle Street. It was built in the early 1930s and has an art deco appearance. (*Keith W. Jones*)

5

Transport & War

The toll house, dated 1831, at Pen-y-Pound in 2003. (*Trevor Scott*)

TRANSPORT

Travel in days gone by was a cumbersome affair. Roads tended to be poor until turnpike companies were formed to build new routes and improve existing ones.

The canal that connects Brecon with the Monmouthshire waterway was built between 1793 and 1812. Canals such as the Mon and Brec, as it is known, were once vital arteries for industry and agriculture. Heavily loaded barges drawn by horses moved vast amounts of coal, iron, limestone and timber until the new steam railways in the mid-1850s took away most of the canal trade. The Newport, Abergavenny & Hereford Railway Co. was formed in 1845 by Act of Parliament to construct a railway between Hereford and Pontypool to link up with the Monmouthshire Railway Co. line from Pontypool to Newport. The NAH company absorbed the Llanvihangel, Grosmont and Hereford tram roads which operated between Abergavenny and Hereford and sometimes used the existing route. The line was opened in 1854 and in 1860 it was taken over by the West Midland Railway which in turn was later taken over by Great Western Railway. Abergavenny once had three railway stations – what is now Monmouth Road, Brecon Road and the Junction.

The warehouse at Llanfoist. The warehouse was completed in about 1820 at the end of ironmaster Hill's primitive horse-drawn railway from Blaenavon to the Brecknock & Abergavenny Canal wharf at Llanfoist. The route includes connections to the limestone quarries at Pwll-Du and Tyla and to the forge at Garn-Ddyrys. A series of counter-balanced inclined planes took the tram road down the mountain to Llanfoist. (*Trevor Scott*)

Horse-drawn barges were used for pleasure trips in the Edwardian age, as this picture shows. (*Bill Roberts*)

The last train from Abergavenny to Merthyr waved through the tunnels at Clydach by onlookers on 5 January 1958. (*Keith W. Jones*)

The last train from Abergavenny to Merthyr left on Sunday 5 January 1958. A special locomotive had been brought out by the Stephenson Locomotive Society for the occasion. The line and its branches were among the most scenically spectacular and had the steepest gradients in the British Isles. Their origins were in the earliest tram roads. The line was built in the nineteenth century to gain access to the lucrative region of South Wales where the coal mines and iron works were experiencing rapid expansion. (*Romley Marney*)

The railway bridge at Pen-y-Pound before demolition. (*Keith W. Jones*)

End of an era. The dismantling of the locomotive sheds at Brecon Road. The site also had a turntable for trains. (*Keith W. Jones*)

WARTIME

Troops leaving Monmouth Road station during the First World War. The town was used as a base for some of the Welsh Army Corps who came for their military training. The men were billeted with local families. (*Pamela Mason*)

The Abergavenny branch of the TA, 21 June 1924. It was made up of men from the *Abergavenny Chronicle*, Seargeants Bros' and Dover's printing works. The men include Bert Kennett (back row, right), Harry Cooper, Jack Gouge, Bill Nicholas, Bert Greenwood, Mervin Dunn, Bert Lewis, Oliver Roper, Bill Heath, Mr Taylor, Charlie Rossner and Charlie's brother. (*Pamela Mason*)

During the Second World War Abergavenny was like a garrison town. Many of the larger buildings and houses were taken over by the military and used for offices or accommodation. At Claremont, included in the 'A' branch of Western Command in April 1944 were: Eunice Gilbert (in civvies), Vernon Lee, J.G. Halstead, S.M. Boyle, E. Littlehales, Yvonne Fahy, Betty Hirons, L.C. Newman, K.D. Law, P.E.A. Oxley, S Jenkins, J.M. Ward, Frances Sadleir, V. Francis Scully, F.G.A. Tubb, Margaret Batty, Peggy Latham, M. Lewis Muriel Dent, Joan Peck, Bobbie Stainforth, Gwen M. Ashfield, Rita Huish and Kos Sitwell. (*Eunice Gilbert*)

The Abergavenny Wardens Service, Post A, 2 October 1944. Back row, left to right: Sergeant J. Walby J.I. Parsons, J.S. Humphreys, T.J. Price, A.V. Pavord (Divisional Warden), H. Gardner, W.O. Parry (war reserve), Superintendent A. Briggs. Front row: G. Allen, S.V. Allen, T.J. Evans, J. Barry and S.J. Davies. (*E. Harrington*)

6

Youth & Education

The 5th Abergavenny Girl Guides during a civic parade in 1969. (*Janet Patrick*)

SCOUTS & GUIDES

Govilon Brownies celebrate their tenth anniversary in 1989 at the village hall. (*Oswald Jones*)

Abergavenny Cub Pack, *c.* 1966. The back row includes Steven Butler, Tim Lloyd, Mrs Betty Adams (akela); the centre row includes Keith Francis, Steven Harris, Rhys Morgan; and the front row includes Philip Hemmings, Tony Flynn and David Parker. (*Tony Flynn*)

The Tredilion Cub Pack, 1954. (*Maureen Griffiths*)

SCHOOLS

In 2003 primary and infant schools in Abergavenny underwent a review by Monmouthshire County Council which has drawn up plans to reorganise the education system. Despite opposition from some parents, plans have been put forward to close down two infant schools and relocate other schools. The final decision will be made by the Welsh Assembly Government.

Abergavenny's oldest school is King Henry VIII which was founded in 1542. The grammar school was named after its benefactor, who also appointed its first headmaster, Richard Oldsworthy. The headmaster was paid the annual salary of £13 6s 8d. The school had twenty-six pupils, all boys aged between seven and fourteen. Their day started at 6 a.m. (7 a.m. in winter) and lessons continued until 11 a.m.; the afternoon session ran from 1 p.m. to 6 p.m. (5 p.m. in winter). In 1664 management of the school passed to Jesus College, Oxford, and under a 1760 Act of Parliament the old school building and the tower were pulled down and replaced. At the same time a new house was built for the headmaster. The Georgian building was sold to the freemasons after the Pen-y-Pound school was erected in 1898.

Pupils of King Henry VIII School in 1898, the year when the school moved from St John's to Pen-y-Pound. (*Abergavenny Museum*)

A King Henry VIII School cricket team in the 1930s. The teachers are Mr Newcombe, head of the grammar school, and Mr Porter, head of sports.

The former King Henry VIII School in Pen-y-Pound was vacated in 1972 when a new school was built in Old Hereford Road after the introduction of comprehensive education. It is now a base for the Gwent Theatre and Gwent Young People's Theatre. In addition it houses Gwent Careers Office. Adult education classes are also held here. (*Trevor Scott*)

Abergavenny High School for Girls in 1946: Gwyneth Watkins, Patrician Pearson, Mary Gunter, Audrey Reynolds, Olwen Jones, Marjorie Morris, Jean Drew, Mary Beverley-Burton, Greta Beardsmore, Jeanne Pothecary, Miss Dean, Kathleen Gray, Marguerite Built, Margaret Wycherly, Maureen Silverthorne, Muriel Jones, Anne Murray, Pamela Harris. (*Maureen Griffiths*)

Pupils at the Roman Catholic school, which was for a time in Pen-y-Pond. It is now part of the Ty'r Morwydd environmental study centre. The school closed in 1971. (*Janet Patrick*)

Pupils at Grofield School in Victoria Street in 1953. (*Abergavenny Museum*)

Former pupils and teachers at the unveiling of a plaque to mark the site of the former Grofield School which closed down in 1972 after the introduction of the comprehensive school system. Now the site is a housing complex. Pupils remember the school with great affection, despite having to visit up to eleven different sites to attend classes and sports lessons during the 1950s and 1960s. (*I.M. Morgan*)

Children at Llanarth School, 1925/6. (*Abergavenny Museum*)

Hitting the right notes. The orchestra from Harold Road Junior School in 2000/1. (*South Wales Argus*)

This is our school badge! The St David's Junior School badge may stay the same but the school is likely to be relocated in 2005–6 under Monmouthshire County Council's strategic review of primary education. The new school will be on the site of the Llwynu Infants School building which will be demolished if proposals go ahead. The present open-plan St David's School building is then likely to be converted for use by the Welsh school, Ysgol Gymraeg y Fenni. (*South Wales Argus*)

Pupils from Llwynu Infants School in the 1970s. (*Llwynu Infants School*)

Llanover School in the late 1950s. (*Albert McNab*)

Llanfoist Village School children at the opening of the Safeway store in Llanfoist, 28 February 1997. The children are burying a time capsule to mark the opening. (*Llanfoist Village School*)

Castle Street School in 1899. Note the hoops the children are holding with a ribbon and a bell on each. (*Eddie Madge*)

Victoria School Group 2, *c.* 1922. The headmaster, William Rosser, is on the right. (*Abergavenny Museum*)

Hereford Road Boys School, *c. 1931*. Ken Garland is second in the back row. The headteacher, William Rosser, is on the right. (*Abergavenny Museum*)

Park Street Infants School celebrates St David's Day. Park Street was under threat of closure under schools' reorganisation plans but seems likely to remain open. In May 2003, governors decided to go ahead with an application to turn it from a local education authority controlled school into a voluntary-aided Church in Wales one. The school was founded as a church school in 1894. (*Park Street Infants School*)

ADULT EDUCATION

The Hill Education & Conference Centre. Since 1997 the Hill, part of Coleg Gwent, has established itself as a centre specialising in information technology, Welsh language and horticulture. In addition, the Hill offers a wide range of weekend courses and summer schools. Following a £1½m refurbishment programme, the Hill was re-launched in May 2003 as The Hill Education & Conference Centre.

The Hill mansion was owned by the Lloyd family in the eighteenth century but in 1776 it was bought by William Morgan. William Lloyd Powell bought the estate in 1849. In 1901 on his retirement, Edward Pritchard Martin purchased the estate for £10,000. The estate extended from almost the centre of Abergavenny to the slopes of the Deri. Herbert Clarke Lewis, the second Baron Lewis of Merthyr, purchased the estate in 1918 as a home for his three unmarried sisters, Lilian, Anne and Gwendoline.

On the death of Lilian in 1964, the estate passed to Monmouthshire County Council and was established as a residential centre providing educational courses. In April 1995 The Hill was purchased by Gwent Tertiary College (now Coleg Gwent), Wales's largest educational institution. (*Coleg Gwent*)

7

Sport

First past the post – General beats Dearest Mae and Ploughboy in the 1853 Abergavenny Steeplechase. The other horses were Doe, Harkaway, Nun, Pontiff, Thurgarton and Physician. In the early days races were still being held while golf was played. A large iron grandstand stood near the River Usk and the greens had to be fenced off. In April 1872 the National Hunt Chase was run there and was won by the Red Nob, owned by Mr Sankey and ridden by Captain Holyoake. The National Hunt Chase was held each year at different venues before moving in 1911 to its permanent home at Cheltenham. Traces of Abergavenny's grandstand can still be seen near the sixth tee at the Monmouthshire Golf Club, which was founded in 1892. (*Monmouthshire Golf Club*)

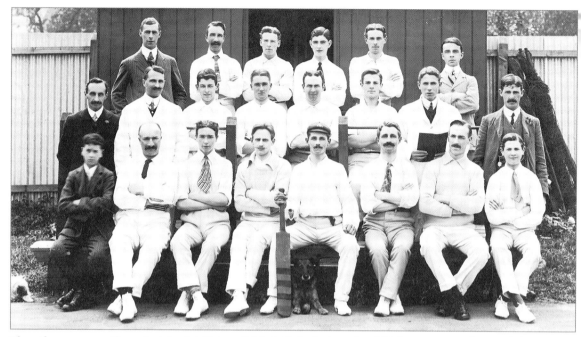

The Abergavenny Shop Assistants' Union Cricket Club during the 1912 season. Back row, left to right: R. Day, T. Gill, A.W. Wozencroft, R. Howells, F. Groves, W.T. Davis (Secretary). Middle row: C. Powell, H. Bullen, J. Stoneham, H. Edwards, R.A. Wintle, J.E. Bush, E. Pierce, E. Bush. Front row: F. Bowen, H. Hunt, E. Gwenlan, R. J. Harrhy, F.H. Turle (Captain) T. Williams, C. Bunce and W. White. (*W. Shackleton*)

A team from Abergavenny Cricket Club at a 1975 benefit match. (*Abergavenny Cricket Club*)

The Abergavenny Cricket Club first XI at the start of the 2003 season. Back row, left to right: John Newall, James Didcote, John Phillips, Ben Powell, Ioan Lilly, James Hrastelj. Front row: Kyle Holmes, Andrew Coles, Keith Newell (captain), Gavin Heritage, Marke Coles. (*Helen Brown*)

ABERGAVENNY CRICKET CLUB

Abergavenny Cricket Club was established in 1834 and is one of the oldest clubs in Wales. It also has one of the most picturesque grounds in Britain.

Before 1896 the club played on a number of pitches around the town from the Castle Meadows by the River Usk to a site that became the livestock market. In 1884 the team played at Bailey Park and then, thanks to the generosity of the Marquess of Abergavenny, the club acquired a 4½-acre field at Avenue Road and Pen-y-Pound which has been its home ever since.

At the beginning of the twentieth century a surge of interest in cricket led to the formation of a number of teams. These included the Shop Assistants' Union Cricket Club, which was later absorbed into the Abergavenny club. This was also the start of the Shackleton family's involvement – three generations have been associated with the club.

In 1977 a fire severely damaged the pavilion but fortunately a Welsh Sports Council grant helped to pay for a larger replacement tea-room. For a time Glamorgan County Cricket Club staged first-class matches at the ground. Worcestershire and Gloucestershire were regular visitors, drawing in spectators from all over the country.

The club has a fine record in supplying players for the first-class game. Perhaps the most famous was Malcolm Nash who had a successful eighteen-year career with Glamorgan. His brother Colin and his father Ted also played for Abergavenny. In 1997 Mike Powell, who also played for Abergavenny, scored 200 not out on his first-class debut for Glamorgan v Oxford University and has now established himself in the county's middle order batting. Both his father and uncle have also long been associated with the Abergavenny club. Wicket-keeper Mark Wallace is the most recent graduate to Glamorgan.

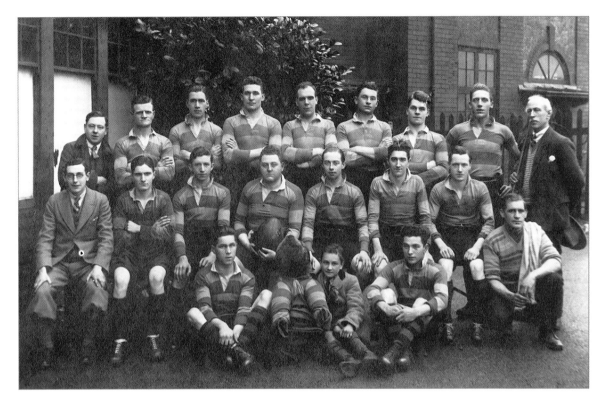

Abergavenny Rugby Football Club 1927/8. C. Watkins (attendant), N. Liddington, V. Lewis, K. Salmon, F. Williams, R. Lewis, A. Snelling, W. Edwards, G. Morgan (linesman). Middle row: E.N.D. Williams (Honorary Secretary), V.R. Davidson, W. Phillips, B. Williams (Captain), J.R. Williams, G. Parsons, R. Jones, W. Pritchard. Front row: C. Morgan, mascot and boy, J. Morgan. (*J.E. Thomas*)

Abergavenny Rugby Football Club, winners of the Ben Francis Cup in 1987 and Monmouthshire RFU champions in 1988. (*Malcolm Lewis*)

Abergavenny Rugby Football Club in 2003. (*Malcolm Lewis*)

ABERGAVENNY RUGBY FOOTBALL CLUB

Abergavenny Rugby Football Club was formed in 1875, although earlier forms of rugby were played in the town during the 1860s. The rules of the game were standardised in about 1871. The club played at Castle Meadows but its first permanent ground was at Ysguborwen Fields, the Pen-y-Pound end of Park Crescent. Then after some seasons at the Fairfield the club started playing on the council pitch in Bailey Park in the 1890s. It has remained there ever since. Until the clubhouse was built in 1960, teams relied on the facilities of pubs and even, from 1924–8, a mortuary in Slaughterhouse Lane.

A number of distinguished players have gone on to win caps for Wales and life member Ken Hewitt was appointed to the general committee of the Welsh Rugby Union in 1993. The club has won the Ben Francis Cup on a number of occasions and took the Monmouthshire Union Premier Division title in the 1987/8 season. There are two teams at senior level, a youth side and teams ranging from under-8s to under-16s.

Abergavenny Thursdays AFC in
the 1940s. (*Abergavenny
Thursdays*)

Abergavenny Thursdays during
2003. (*Trevor Scott*)

ABERGAVENNY THURSDAYS AFC

Abergavenny Thursdays AFC has a long and proud tradition. It is thought the club
was founded in about 1900 by local traders. Thursday was early-closing day and a
number of clubs at the time incorporated the tag in their name. Until the early
1990s the club was one of the more successful outfits within Welsh football. But
since then there has been a fall from grace.

In 1991/2 the club won the Welsh League for the second year in succession and
for the fourth time overall. The club was one of the founders of the League of Wales
in about 1992/3. But since then the club's fortunes have changed and in 2003 it
was relegated to the third division of the Gwent County league. In an effort to reverse
the decline, the club has launched a youth programme in the hope that interest will
be regenerated and will lead to a more successful future.

Abergavenny Rangers Thursday AFC, 1908/9 season. Back row, left to right: W. Brown (Chairman), S. Gumm (committee), T.H. Maxwell (Treasurer), T. Walkley. Second row: C. James, (trainer), C. Bailey, A. Pitt, W.H. Jones, J. Roberts, F. Martin (Honorary Secretary). Seated: E. Denner (committee), S. Breeze, W. Morgan (Vice-Captain), E. Williams (Captain), W. Denner, A. Williams, H. Lyons (committee). Front: W. Knight and Watkins. (*H. Shackleton*)

The Fireflies, winners of the Leo Fine Challenge Cup in the six-a-side soccer competition held during the Abergavenny Carnival festivities in 1949. The team was made up mainly of Abergavenny firemen. Back row, left to right: J. Staniland, Vasa Kovandzich, L. Breeze. Seated: Vin Sullivan, H.G. Owen (President), B. Symonds (Captain), Mrs P. Telford (the Mayoress) and Steve Hornby. (*E. Harrington*)

Mardy AFC, 1999. The club was founded in 1897 and was the first in the history of the Gwent Central
League to win Divisions 1 and 2 and the cup in the same season – 1993/4. The name of Malcolm 'Macky'
Skinner (second right, back row) has been synonymous with the club for more than forty years.
In its centenary year – 1997 – he was made a life member along with Dennis Bailey, Colin Thomas and
Arthur Stent. (*Malcolm Lewis*)

Mardy AFC has a strong youth policy. Here are the members of the junior section with their tally of medals
in about the year 2000. (*Malcolm Lewis*)

The girls' six-a-side soccer team from Abergavenny Youth Club, 1953. Front row, left to right: Mary Baker, Mary Norton. Middle row: June Hodges, Nina Bowen, Val Powell. Back row: Mr Bartlett (youth warden), Shirley Jones, Mr G. Walbyoff (trainer). (*Abergavenny Museum*)

The gymnastics display team from Abergavenny senior youth club in 1953 with youth warden, Mr Bartlett, and instructor, Mr Walbyoff. (*Romley Marney*)

During the mid-1960s, the Welsh Motor Show was staged at the Market Hall. Pictured here is a young Peter Law (standing), now a member of the Wales National Assembly, and journalist Don Chambers (in car) Secretary of Abergavenny Auto Club, which organised the event annually for five years. On show were the latest models from the British Motor Co., rally cars and vintage cars. There was a special appearance by the car from the film *Chitty Chitty Bang Bang*. Among the club's members is Nicky Grist, one of the most successful world rallying co-drivers ever. (*Armour PR*)

The motorcycling section of the Abergavenny Auto Club during one of their events. (*Abergavenny Auto Club*)

A paraglider's view of the River Usk near the bridge at Llanfoist. Before the Bailey Park pool was built in 1939, swimming lessons were given at the old lido by the side of the river. (*Christopher White*)

The lifeguards at Bailey Park Pool with the Deri Mountain in the background, 1982. (*Sandra Probert*)

Abergavenny Badminton Club in 1989 after one of its most successful seasons. The ladies' team won League Division 3 and the mixed 'B' side won Division 5 in the Gwent Badminton League. (*Oswald Jones*)

Abergavenny Tennis Club bought its present premises in Pen-y-Pound in 1923. Since then the club, which has 104 junior and 101 senior members, has extended its facilities with the help of lottery grants. The club now has two floodlit carpet courts, three tarmac doubles courts, a singles court, three mini courts and a practice wall. (*Trevor Scott*)

The Abergavenny Bowling Club, 1989. The club, founded in 1860, is one of the oldest in Wales. The original green was at the Great Western Hotel near what is now the Monmouth Road railway station. It was then named the Little Skirrid Club. The Avenue Road greens were opened in 1910. The club has a copy of a report of a match played against Cardiff in 1878. In 1989 the club won the Monmouthshire Bowls Association Championships when members beat Beaufort at Ebbw Vale in the final. (*Oswald Jones*)

The Nevill Ladies' Bowling Club at the Avenue Road ground in 1993. (*Malcolm Lewis*)

The Bailey Park Bowling Club in 1985. Back row, left to right: Ken Whittaker, Gordon Rees, Peter Fitzpatrick, Lionel Price, Tim Rees. Front row: Dai Davies, Darren Price, Fred Diggins, Irvin Jenkins, Brian Sanders, Lynn Knight. The club was formed in 1924 and numbers internationals among its past players, including John Anstey, whose father Don and son Mark also played for the club. (*Bailey Park Bowling Club*)

The South Wales and Mon League-winning team from Bailey Park ladies' section, 1992. Back row, left to right: Joan Rickets, Myra Jenkins, Joan Rutter, Glenys Fitzpatrick, Brenda Fitzpatrick, Flo Watkins, Rachel Bull, Molly Preece. Front row: Gaynor Davies, Ceridwen McCarthy, Deana Jones (captain), Shirley Sutherland. (*Bailey Park Bowling Club*)

e two-week eleventh Abergavenny Pool Festival attracted teams from all over Wales in 2003. Here are
even-year-old Amy Smith, the Abergavenny junior champion and ladies' champion, with Zara Rogers,
dies' singles' runner-up, and Stacey Warner, junior singles' runner-up. With them is the Welsh Ladies'
am manager Jan Madden. Amy's decider in an Abergavenny ladies' team v Wales ladies' game gave her
ree wins from four – and the player of the day trophy. (*Lynne Smith*)

iger Iris Williams with a team from the Usk and district pool league at the Savaas Club in 1991–2. The
iyers are Paul Thomas, Vaughan Greaves, Des Hughes, John Maule, Adrian Hancock, Kevin Cartright,
ve Skinner and Richard Gunter. (*Steve Skinner*)

Abergavenny Hockey Club, 2003. Abergavenny was once known as the premier hockey town of Wales. Th club was founded in October 1897 and has had a number of players picked to represent Wales. Dr 'Bi Griffiths played for Great Britain in the 1948 Olympics. Stan Hall, Chris Holland, Billy Denner, Acker Shar and Jack Jonathon all represented Wales, and Philip Jones won a schoolboy cap. (*Malcolm Lewis*)

Abergavenny Road Club member Nicholas Kenwright sets the pace. The club was founded in 1979 and membership soon increased to accommodate all types of cycling from racing to touring. There is also a thriving mountain bike section. In 1987 three Abergavenny youngsters, Nicholas Bailey, Peter Legg and Gordon Main, won th National Schoolboys' Time Trial Championship. Member Richard Wooles ro for Wales and has become an Olympic coac for Britain's women's road race team. He also coached Wales to first place in the women's road race at the Commonwealth Games in 2002. Another member is the British Road Race 2002 champion Julian Winn. (*Terry Williamson*)

Above: The Nevill Hall snooker team who won the local league in about 1992. From left to right: Richard C. Shaw, Paul Hopkins (team supporter), Daniel O'Connell, Brian Watkins, Mark Watkins, Dennis Kirby, Richard Shaw, Phil Jones, Darren Price. (*Richard C. Shaw*)

Glyn Williams, born in 1911. A keen all-round sportsman, he played football and cricket locally, and reached the semi-finals of the Welsh amateur boxing championship in the bantamweight class in about 1927. (*Glyn Williams*)

ACKNOWLEDGEMENTS

Special thanks should go to the following people: Frank Olding, Gwyn Jones, Rachael Rogers (Curator of Abergavenny Museum), Sally Davis, Janet Herrod, Abergavenny Museum staff and Monmouthshire County Council, Richard Davies, Trevor Scott for doing most of the modern day photography, the committee and members of Abergavenny Local History Society, Keith W. Jones and the Abergavenny Steam Society, Malcolm Lewis, Mrs Joan Marney for the use of her late husband Rowley Marney's photographs and Chris Hall, executor of photographer Oswald 'Ossie' Jones's estate.

Thanks must also go to Betty Ambler, Andre Arkell, Frances Baines, Jenny Barnes, Joan Bell, Sheila Bevan, Michael Blackmore, Kay Blackwell, David Bowen, Helen Brown, Stan Brown, Don Chambers, Edna and Douglas Edwards, Lesley and Tony Flynn, Eunice Gilbert, Maureen Griffiths, Sheila Holloway, Kyle Holmes, Steve Hornby, Joan Isaac, Phil Jones, Ken Key, Edna Lewis, Albert NcNab, Margaret and Pat Martin, Pamela Mason, the Revd Roy Matthews, Janet Patrick, Sandra Probert, Bill Roberts, Brian Shackleton, Ian Shackleton, Richard C. Shaw, Malcolm Skinner, Steve Skinner, John Straker, Richard and Angela Vaughan, Derrick Watkins, Gareth Webb, Christopher White, Jane White, Mary White, Paddy Wills-Wood, the Revd Canon Jeremy Winston, Abergavenny Auto Club, Abergavenny Borough Band, Abergavenny Bowls Club and Nevill Ladies' Bowls, Abergavenny branch of the WRVS, Abergavenny Chamber of Trade, *Abergavenny Chronicle*, Abergavenny Cricket Club, Abergavenny Hockey Club, Abergavenny Library staff, Abergavenny Light Opera, Abergavenny Operatic and Dramatic Society, Abergavenny Pantomime Society, Abergavenny Road Club, Abergavenny Rugby Club, Abergavenny Tennis Club, Abergavenny Thursdays AFC, Bailey Park Bowling Club and ladies' section, Gwent Bach Society, Gwent Singers, Gwent Theatre, head teachers of local schools, League of Nevill Hall Friends, Monmouthshire Golf Club, Nevill Hall Sound, Paraventure Extreme Sports, Redrow Homes and Graham Frecknall, *South Wales Argus* and *Abergavenny Free Press*, South Wales Shire Horse Society, the Warden of Llandovery College, and everyone else who helped.

FURTHER READING

Abergavenny Local History Society, *A Town Remembers: Memories of Wartime Abergavenny 1939–1945*, Abergavenny Local History Society, 2nd edn, 2003
——, *Street Survey of Abergavenny*, reference only
Davies, Dr John, *The Making of Wales*, Sutton Publishing, 1996 and 1999
Davies, Richard, *A Church, Two Chapels and a School*, 1999
——, *And So To School*, 2000
Howell, Raymond, *A History of Gwent*, Gomer Press, 1992
Jones, Gwyn (with illustrations by Michael Blackmore), *A Walk around Abergavenny*, 1990
——, (mainly illustrated by Michael Blackmore), *Medieval Town and Market of Abergavenny*
——, *Prehistoric Abergavenny*
——, *Roman Abergavenny*, 1982
——, *Medieval Abergavenny*, 1984
Olding, Frank, *The Prehistoric Landscapes of the Eastern Black Mountains*, Archaeopress (BAR 297), 2000
——, *Vanished Abergavenny – Y Fenni Ddiflanedig*, Sutton Publishing, 1994